Playing Among the Stars

Playing Among the Stars

Conversations with
Damien Chazelle

Nathan Réra

Sticking Place Books
New York

Cover image: Damien Chazelle on the set of *First Man* © Daniel McFadden

© 2023 Rouge Profond, Aix-en-Provence
Jouer parmi les étoiles: Conversations avec Damien Chazelle

Translation by Paul Cronin
© Sticking Place Books 2024
www.stickingplacebooks.com

Designed by Goran Tovilovic

All rights reserved.
No part of this book may be reproduced, stored in or introduced into a retrieval system, or transmitted, in any form or by any means (electronic, mechanical, photocopying, recording or otherwise) without the written permission of the publishers, except in the case of brief quotations embodied in critical articles or reviews.

ISBN 978-1-942782-42-1

For Ennio

Make 'em laugh
Make 'em laugh
Don't you know everyone wants to laugh?
(Ha ha!)

>Arthur Freed
>& Nacio Herb Brown, 1952

Fly me to the moon
Let me play among the stars

>Bart Howard, 1954

CONTENTS

With Flying Colours	1
Practising Scales First home movies and *Guy and Madeline on a Park Bench*	11
Finding the Right Tempo On various screenplays	33
Faster Than Music *Whiplash*	43
Dancing Among the Stars *La La Land*	67
A Trip to the End of the Moon *First Man*	91
Another Tempo *The Eddy*	115
In Search of Lost Time *Babylon*	127
Coda	151
Lyrics	161
Acknowledgements	169
Index	171

WITH FLYING COLOURS

Many directors have engaged in a sustained dialogue about their work[1] at a relatively advanced stage of their careers, once their place in film history has been established. Proposing such a thing to a filmmaker aged just 37, whose body of work comprises "only" five feature films and a miniseries, doesn't necessarily come naturally and might even appear premature. Yet already in the first act of his career, Damien Chazelle is proving himself to be a director who doesn't just have "ideas," but a "philosophy,"[2] as evidenced by the coherence of his short but dense filmography, which will be explored alongside the man himself in the pages that follow.

Since my discovery of *Whiplash* in Aix-en-Provence cinema with (could one dream of a more auspicious start?) my publisher and accomplice Guy Astic, Chazelle's work has continuously drawn me into its vortex of images, music and sounds, my interest increasing with each successive film. Awarded an Oscar for Best Director[3] for *La La Land*, his greatest public and critical success to date, at just 32 years old, I wondered whether the young Franco-American director would invent himself anew or, at the risk of losing sight of his style and soul, instead be absorbed by the Hollywood machine and involve himself in trendy projects. His next feature, *First Man*, erased all doubts I might have had. The challenging task of narrating one of the great American success stories as a tragedy was coupled with an aesthetic challenge that not only opened up his work in new directions but illuminated it with a fresh new light. This misunderstood film confirmed that Chazelle, American filmmaker, is carving a singular path, while successfully avoiding being pigeonholed by critics. *The Eddy*, one of the most original series of recent years, followed by *Babylon*, a stunning epic fresco about the transition from silent to sound cinema, only amplified the reach of his artistic gesture and cemented his place among the most stimulating and puzzling filmmakers of the twenty-first century.

If Damien Chazelle's work is subject to criticism and sometimes causes confusion, it's because it is in perpetual redefinition, animated by conflicting currents which make it difficult to pin down. With his first feature in 2009, *Guy and Madeline on a Park Bench*, a romance between a student and a black trumpet player in Boston, Chazelle was audacious in blending reality and artifice. Largely improvised and shot with a handheld camera with non-professional actors, the film lies somewhere between Frederick Wiseman's observational cinema and John Cassavetes' *Shadows*, while incorporating song and dance sequences that pay homage to Hollywood's great musical classics, as well as the films of Jacques Demy. *Guy and Madeline on a Park Bench* draws on various jazz repertoires, while leaning towards swing. The music and songs composed by Justin Hurwitz are openly inspired by American jazz standards and Michel Legrand's melodies, and also celebrate the spirit of bebop – elements of which Chazelle integrates into the film.[4]

Jazz is, once again, a focal point in *Whiplash*. Set at a prestigious conservatory in New York, the film explores the ambiguous relationship between Andrew Neiman, a young drummer who dreams of being Buddy Rich, and Terence Fletcher, his teacher, who vacillates between praise and intense criticism of his playing. Chazelle made a clean break in his filmmaking, moving from a free, experimental style to a highly structured one. Aiming for a certain formal purity, scripted and directed with metronomic precision, virtuosic in how it connects the musical with the psychological thriller, *Whiplash* leaves no room for chance or accident – values that *Guy and Madeline on a Park Bench* elevated. This aesthetic reversal is accompanied by an antithetical representation of music. The love for jazz, which infused every frame of *Guy and Madeline*, is now tinged with bitterness: exhausting rehearsals, power struggles between musicians, performance anxiety, and the solitude of the instrumentalist all temper the joy of playing – without, however, diminishing the pleasure that simply listening to the film delivers. Although the jazz community thought it necessary to criticise the film because it perpetuated certain clichés,[5] Chazelle was aiming less to paint a realistic picture of American jazz schools than deliver a parable on the price we pay to achieve our dreams, as inspired by his own experience as a drummer. In his late teens, Damien Chazelle lived the life of a musician, like a caterpillar in its chrysalis, before undergoing a transformation into a filmmaker. Retrospectively, *Guy and Madeline on a Park Bench* reveals itself to be a film about this metamorphosis. Chazelle briefly appears on screen, teaching the basics of drumming to the main protagonist, before definitively exchanging his drumsticks for a camera.

However, unlike Maurice Pialat, who repeated that he would have "liked to be a painter, even a mediocre one, rather than a filmmaker, even a great one," Chazelle never considered cinema a fallback. His musical training was merely a detour, intended to strengthen his primary calling: filmmaking. But it was crucial in shaping the direction of his work, which, from its inception, has been dedicated to exploring the glowing bonds between image and music. Borrowing Gilles Mouëllic's formulation, it might be said that for Chazelle, filming music is akin to "capturing a cinematic ideal."[6] The camera – often in motion – eagerly documents the musicians' movements, the precision mechanics, and the gleam of their instruments, as evidenced by the recurring close-ups which have become a signature of his work, of the engulfing brass, as if the camera is diving down into the inner workings of the music. Nevertheless, Chazelle's films derive their aesthetic singularity not only from the image but from the organic connection between it and the music, as evidenced by the special bond he has forged with Justin Hurwitz, who, with each film, begins composing at an early stage of the creative process.

La La Land, Damien Chazelle's third feature film, accomplishes the feat of "reconciling the public"[7] with the musical while also advancing the ideas found in *Guy and Madeline on a Park Bench*. The film tells the story of the encounter between two people pursuing their dreams: Sebastian (Ryan Gosling), a cash-strapped jazz pianist who hopes to open his own club, and Mia (Emma Stone), a young waitress who undergoes humiliating auditions in the hope of making it as an actress. Both achieve their dreams but sacrifice their love on the altar of success. Peppered with cinematic references, like motifs in a Persian carpet, *La La Land* asserts itself as the swan song of the Golden Age of Hollywood musicals. In his quest to recapture the genre's lost innocence, Chazelle acknowledges that nothing will ever be the same again. *La La Land*, in this sense, possesses the beauty of the final bursts of a firework display which, in the wake of the grand finale, descends, while illuminating the night sky with its dying glow.

Following his jazz trilogy, Chazelle temporarily left behind the musical to explore the historical epic, tackling one of the biggest stories there is: the first steps taken by Neil Armstrong on the Moon. The culmination of a series of films about space exploration, *First Man* sets itself apart because it delves less into the Apollo mission and more into the notion that our hero – subtly portrayed by Ryan Gosling – finds it impossible to continue living after the loss of his child. The hints of melancholy in Chazelle's films, usually tempered by the energy and jubilation they emit, are instead powerfully acute in *First Man*, and the audience is invited to become part of a deeply personal and painful experience. At first glance, this austere and serious film feels out of place within Chazelle's body of work, but it actually revolves around one of his favourite themes: the creation, evolution and circulation of images. The Moon, as a "site of projection

– dreams and fantasies, rockets and bodies – at the heart of cinematic spectacle since the late nineteenth century"[8] is something Damien Chazelle, a knowledgeable cinephile, is acutely aware of.

Moreover, *First Man* gives the director the opportunity to develop a key concept in his work, that of transcendence, which was at the core of *Whiplash* and *La La Land*, and reaches its peak in *Babylon*. Perhaps it was less about seeing *Whiplash* as a reflection of the Darwinian notion of survival of the fittest, as lazily reiterated by the press, and more a variation on Nietzsche's concept of the "superman." Following the film's release, Chazelle spoke of the "existential rage" driving his characters, which, he said, stemmed from them not being "supermen."[9] Aware of their imperfect, even worthless, nature, Chazelle's characters strive to rise above their lowly condition and reach for an ideal of perfection, and thus – like Icarus, who flew too close to the sun[10] – risk burning their wings. In Andrew Neiman and Neil Armstrong, as well as pianist Elliot (André Holland) in *The Eddy* and idealistic Manny (Diego Calva) and uncontrollable Nellie (Margot Robbie) in *Babylon*, are elements of the "great egoism" described by Nietzsche: "It operates beyond good and evil, ready, in pursuit of its values, to sacrifice others or even oneself. It chooses to expose itself and live dangerously for the sake of its creation."[11]

The Promethean destiny of the Chazelle hero hinges on mastery of technique – whether musical, acting or scientific. It is what enables them to break out from their natural environment and shoot for the stars, symbolically in *Whiplash*, *La La Land* and *Babylon*, literally in *First Man*, where astronauts are shown "doing what all ages before ours have thought to be the exclusive prerogative of divine action."[12]

Following *First Man*, Chazelle's journey took him to Paris, where he had the opportunity to create his first television series, rekindle his connection with jazz, and revisit the traces of his adolescence, when he roamed from cinema to cinema nurturing his cinephilia. A collective work born of healthy rivalry between musicians and filmmakers, *The*

Eddy is nonetheless a thematic and stylistic encapsulation of Chazelle's work, a reflection on the act of creation, on the blurring of boundaries between musician and actor, documentary and fiction, improvisation and the blending of genres.

At the end of this interlude, which temporarily diverted him from filmmaking, Chazelle embarked on his fifth feature, *Babylon* – an epic, more than three hours long, which takes in a major chapter of Hollywood history, from the end of the silent era to the revolution of talkies, combining a myriad of characters, mixing burlesque comedy and tragedy.

With its Griffith-like excesses and Leone-esque breadth, featuring a prestigious cast and an experienced crew, *Babylon* was announced as Chazelle's most ambitious project to date – a determination seemingly unshaken by the lukewarm critical reception of *First Man*. And yet, a hiccup disrupted the well-oiled machine. A few weeks before filming was to start came the first lockdown, an attempt to curb the spread of the coronavirus epidemic, leading to the film's indefinite postponement. A year and a few months later, after numerous changes to cast and crew, Chazelle finally began filming, almost as if nothing had happened. Only surgical masks on set served as a reminder that *Babylon* is a film of the Covid era. By late October 2021, Chazelle began post-production, unaware that the editing stage would become an extended undertaking, concluding only shortly before the film's release in the United States.

It was during this period that my proposal for this book of interviews reached Chazelle. I dreamed of being able to discuss with him every single question his films sparked in me, hoping that even if he was unable to respond immediately, he might be intrigued by my project and contact me once post-production of his film was done. To my great surprise, it took him less than forty-eight hours to write back, with astounding simplicity: "I'm very happy to receive your message, and I would be delighted to participate in these interviews. It's true that *Babylon* is all consuming at the moment, but I think we will be able to find the time."[13]

As Damien shuttled daily between his home and the editing room in Los Angeles, we quickly agreed that video conferencing would be the most practical way of proceeding, allowing him to participate as his schedule permitted. Beginning in the spring of 2022, we met regularly to discuss his career and body of work, following a chronological progression but always allowing for detours or leaps in time, depending on my questions. Given our small age difference, an informal tone emerged naturally, and our conversations quickly evolved into a fluid and spontaneous dialogue. Due to his paternal origins, Damien generally expressed himself in French, but sometimes switched to English when he lacked the vocabulary to express a certain idea or discuss more technical or theoretical things. Although adjustments were made for the transition from spoken to written form, the interviews retain the conversational dynamic we established from the first minutes of our dialogue.

Throughout the pages, readers will note the obvious intellectual alertness of my interlocutor, who, I must emphasise, never asked that I send my questions in advance and never refused to answer even the most delicate ones. His accessibility and generosity, coupled with his rhetorical skills, contributed to making this work less of a question-and-answer ping-pong between interviewer and interviewee, and more of a genuine dialogue, free from any media constraints, between two enthusiasts of cinema.

In addition to painting a picture of him as a cinephile and aesthete, my conversations with Chazelle underscore how much he asserts himself as a filmmaker of paradox. In his *Philosophical Fragments*, Søren Kierkegaard sees paradox as "the passion of thought."[14] Defining it as "a crucial moment, a pivot," Olivier Abiteboul observes that "the impasse into which it seems to engage designates the limit from which everything can be redefined, reconceived – in short, come into being."[15] I posit that paradox is a fundamental aspect of Chazelle's work. *Whiplash* depicts the musician at work like a boxer in the ring; *La La Land* employs the typically joyful musical genre to portray a story of thwarted love; *First Man* is a triumphant space epic in the mode of failure; *Babylon* celebrates the madness and poetry of Hollywood while simultaneously delivering a ruthless indictment of the place.

It is with *Babylon*, the thread of this book, that I wish to conclude this brief introduction. My discovery of the film in Paris during a special preview was an emotionally charged moment, during which Damien Chazelle and I finally met face to face. It seemed to me that this monumental film, carried by audacity and energy, confirmed Flaubert's famous assertion that one can judge the beauty of a work by the strength of the punches it delivers and the length of time it takes to recover from them.[16] *Babylon* is intoxicating, exhilarating, exhausting, even overwhelming, driven by its author's desire to dynamite the rules and push cinematic language to thrilling extremes. Excess appears as a virtue, citation as an aesthetic value – as was already the case in *La La Land*, but amplified here tenfold. Chazelle employs a form of visual sampling by summoning, in a single impulse, the unruly crowds of Griffith's *Intolerance*, the bacchanals of DeMille's *Manslaughter*, the elephant from Blake Edwards' *The Party*, the showdowns of Coppola's *The Godfather*, the goddesses of Kubrick's *Eyes Wide Shut*, Federico Fellini's festive visions, and the mountains of white powder from De Palma's *Scarface*. *Babylon* derives its originality as much from this baroque fusion as from the glorious and moving dialogue it has with the radiant *Singin' in the Rain*. It is, in fact, a dark, grotesque and decadent version of that film.

The mixed critical reception of *Babylon* ("bloated madness" for some, "a cinematic marvel" for others) prompted me to attempt to probe its stakes in a final chapter that takes the form of an epilogue. Damien Chazelle examines the role of criticism while sketching an overview of cinema in the age of Covid, franchises and streaming platforms. Lucid, but always measured, concerned yet fundamentally optimistic, it is as if he applies to himself the wonderful ethos of Gene Kelly's Don Lockwood in *Singin' in the Rain*, which might also serve as an epigraph for this book: *Dignity, always dignity.*

1. It is important to distinguish between a journalistic interview, intended for publication in the press, typically as part of a film's promotional campaign, and conversations meant to be published as a literary work. It is the latter category of interview which I refer to here.
2. This idea is borrowed from Jean Douchet, in the preface to Jordan Mintzer's *Conversations with James Gray* (Synecdoche, 2011), 13.
3. Chazelle broke the old record for precocity held by Norman Taurog, who won the Oscar for Best Director for his film *Skippy* (1931), at the age of 32 years and 8 months.
4. The filmmaker's reuse of existing themes and motifs aligns his method with that of the boppers. As Laurent de Wilde points out, "the vast majority of bebop themes are based on paraphrasing existing songs: by using the harmonic structure of popular songs of the time, the boppers were more like pirates than composers." From *Monk* (Gallimard, 1996), 39.
5. See, for example, the interview with drummer Peter Erskine by Sean O'Connell (24 February 2015) at www.kcet.org and the review by Tyran Grillo (8 December 2014) at www.allaboutjazz.com.
6. Gilles Mouëllic, "De quelques performances musicales dans le cinéma contemporain" in Séverine Abhervé, N.T. Binh, José Moure (eds.), *Musiques de films: nouveaux enjeux* (Les Impressions nouvelles, 2013), 162.
7. N.T. Binh, "Genre populaire, genre savant? La France et la comédie musicale" in N.T. Binh (ed.), *Comédies musicales, la joie de vivre du cinéma* (Éditions de la Martinière, 2018), 27.
8. Emmanuelle André, *L'Attrait de la Lune* (Éditions Yellow Now, 2020), 6.
9. Emma Brown, "Damien Chazelle and the Limits of Perfection," *Interview*, 8 October 2014.
10. This comparison was made by clinical psychologist Vincent Cornalba in his analysis of *Whiplash*: "La fonction de l'adversité dans le processus adolescent," *Adolescence*, volume 34, number 2, 2016.
11. Gilles Merlio, "Le surhomme nietzschéen: un être singulier ou un exemple pour tous?" in Michel Kauffmann and Rolf Wintermeyer (eds.), *Figures de la singularité* (Presses Sorbonne Nouvelle, 2014), 71-88.
12. Hannah Arendt, *The Human Condition* (Doubleday, 1959), 245.
13. Damien Chazelle, email sent to the author, February 8, 2022.
14. Cited in Olivier Abiteboul, *Le Paradoxe apprivoisé* (Flammarion, 1998), 197.
15. ibid., 75.
16. Gustave Flaubert, letter to Louise Colet, 15 July 1853, in *Correspondance, Troisième série* (1852-1854) (Louis Conard, 1927), 282.

PRACTISING SCALES
First home movies and *Guy and Madeline on a Park Bench*

Damien, today marks the beginning of a series of conversations covering your short but prolific career. When I suggested this book to you, you accepted, without hesitation, to engage in this face-to-face. Should I conclude that, unlike Pasolini, who claimed to "hate" interviews and consented to them "out of pure weakness,"[1] you find something of worth in them?

I have mixed feelings about it. On the one hand, I'm not particularly fond of answering questions, but on the other, I grew up reading interviews with filmmakers. I was eager to hear them talk about their work and explain how they came up with certain ideas or solved certain directorial problems. That's why I did audio commentaries for the DVDs of my films, because I remember how much interviews helped me when I aspired to become a director. One of the sadder ironies of the filmmaker's profession is that among all the people surrounding us on a film set, we're the only ones who never really know how our fellow directors work. Actors, technicians and crew members all move from one set to another, working with different directors, but for us filmmakers, that's not possible. Interviews allow us to break down that barrier.

You're currently deep in post-production on your latest feature, Babylon, *and after our conversation today you'll head back to the editing room. That might make the exercise we're about to engage in even more challenging.*

I feel more relaxed during post-production than during filming. And yet, to be honest, I often feel like I'm in a tunnel. It's very difficult for me to find a balance between film and everyday life. Every time I finish shooting, I start post-production with this fanciful idea that I'll finally have more time, energy and freedom to consider other projects. That was probably my state of mind when you first reached out. [*laughs*] Generally, after each shoot, I like to take a couple of weeks off and forget about the film as best I can, so I can arrive at post-production refreshed and with a clear mind. Right now, apart from our discussions and *Babylon*'s post-production, I don't really have time for anything else. I try to write, to brainstorm – but that's not getting me very far at the moment.

Did the Covid-19 pandemic shake things up in Hollywood?

Not really. We filmed *Babylon* between summer and fall 2021. Covid impacted the shoot a bit more than it did post-production, but the process was basically the same as before the pandemic, despite protocols and increased bureaucracy, which led to additional costs and financial problems. Overall, we had less budgetary flexibility, making things tough for the producers. But when the cameras were rolling it was business as usual. We were lucky to do what we wanted.

In only five feature films, you have managed to establish a truly original style, blending classicism and modernity with coherent threads and recurring themes – which we'll delve into throughout our conversations. But first, I would like to understand how your calling as a filmmaker came about. You were born in 1985 in Providence to an academic family. Your mother Celia is a medieval historian and your father Bernard is one of the pioneers of algorithmic geometry. Everything seemed to point towards an academic career. When did your longing to make films emerge?

I don't recall ever wanting to do anything else. My desire to make films took various forms, depending on the periods of my life and where I was. My earliest memories are more of cartoons than films: Disney's *Cinderella* was the first one I saw on TV, and *Peter Pan* was the first I watched in cinemas, when older Disney titles were re-released. At home, we had a collection of VHS tapes of animated features, and I would ask my parents to play them on repeat. I couldn't read yet, but I learned to draw in response to what I saw on the screen. I quickly envisioned myself as Walt Disney, even though I didn't really know who he was. I was fascinated by the iconic logo that opened his films. When I was old enough to watch live-action movies, the concept of "cinema" became more tangible to me, even though in my mind I didn't really make a clear distinction between being an illustrator, cartoonist, painter or filmmaker.

Your childhood sketchbooks reflect your early talent. At the age of seven or eight, you wrote and illustrated your own stories, in which cinema and music intertwine. One of them, How the First Song Was Written, *was about the planet Melody, where green creatures use musical rhythms as their language. One of the extraterrestrials sneaks to Earth, is imprisoned, and offers to compose a song for his cellmate which is so brilliant that it gets them released. Your "film books" also contained the making of stories of the films you dreamed about. Did you continue drawing after that?*

Not really. I was quite good as a child, but when I got hold of my father's camcorder, I started making home movies, and music came into the picture a few years later. Drawing took a back seat, and I never really got much better than I was in elementary school. These days I do draw my own storyboards, which I did for the entirety of *Whiplash* and a significant portion of *Babylon*, and which I show only to close members of the crew. When I have to communicate with a larger number of technicians or a specific department, like when we shot the space sequences in *First Man* or the big scenes in *Babylon*, I work with a professional storyboard artist who helps turn my sketches or ideas into a more readable, understandable form.

I read that your maternal great-grandfather worked for Paramount Pictures during the silent era.

That's right. As a child, his son, John Martin, my mother's father, acted in a few films.[2]

Did you ever talk about it with your grandfather?

A little, yes. I don't remember long conversations, but it certainly sparked my curiosity. Later on, my grandfather pursued an academic career and became an English professor. His acting talent sometimes resurfaced when he recited poems and delivered long Shakespearean soliloquies.

Maybe that's where your younger sister Anna's calling came from. She's an actress and made brief appearances in La La Land, First Man *and* Babylon.

Perhaps. I cast her in my home movies, along with friends from the neighbourhood. I'm not sure if that's when she caught the acting bug or if she realised later on how deeply drawn she was to acting. She's forging her own path, and not just as an actress. She writes, and is starting to direct, too.

Your parents, apparently disappointed by the education provided to you at Catholic Sunday school, enrolled you in Hebrew school.

That's true. My mother had enrolled me in Confraternity of Christian Doctrine classes because she wanted me to read Bible stories, but she didn't like the education being offered there or other nearby Catholics schools, so she enrolled me in Hebrew school, which was the only remaining option. During the day I attended regular classes at elementary school and then participated in a programme where once a week, in the evening, we read the Bible and learned to read ancient Hebrew. For two years I was the only clandestine Catholic in the room. [*laughs*] When my favourite teacher moved away, I continued with private Hebrew classes for another two years before eventually stopping because I just didn't have time.

Did you ever develop an interest in spiritual or religious matters?

It's difficult for me to answer that question. Religion isn't a subject that attracts me much or inspires me as a filmmaker, but reading the Bible was a foundational experience. I was fascinated by the stories from the Old Testament, like Noah's Ark or the Israelites crossing the Red Sea, fleeing from the Egyptian army. They definitely had an impact on me, much like tales of Greek mythology or the epic *Beowulf*.

Did you enjoy watching historical dramas as a child?

No, I actually disliked that genre. It was so boring! After my fairy-tale phase, I shifted to crime dramas, film noir, Hitchcock films. That's what got me going.

Because of your father, who was born and raised in the Paris region, you have a good command of French. Did you often visit France when you were young?

When I was very young, we spent a whole year in Orsay, and later, every summer, we would vacation in Paris, Normandy and sometimes in the South, where my paternal grandmother was from. When I was twelve or thirteen, my parents took a sabbatical year and we moved to Paris, where my sister and I went to school. So my childhood and adolescence were split between France and New Jersey.

Did your father speak to you in French at home?

Primarily in English. I learned a bit of French during family vacations, but I improved mostly when I was at Collège Sévigné, a private school in Paris.

Paris was an important influence on your love of cinema, right?

Absolutely. There were dozens of classics screened every day in cinemas, and when my school friends went on vacation I was on my own, which is when I stumbled upon [the weekly listing guide] *Pariscope*, which quickly became my bible. Every day I moved from one cinema to another to watch films and explore different neighbourhoods. The irony is that I saw canonical Hollywood works for the first time in Paris, films I had only heard about back home – like *A Streetcar Named Desire*, *Some Like It Hot* and *Bonnie and Clyde*. I had seen bits of *Bonnie and Clyde* on video when I was younger and it didn't particularly interest me. But rediscovering the film on a giant panoramic screen, in a packed cinema in the heart of Paris – that was an extraordinary experience for me. It's when I began to fully appreciate the power of cinema. Later, I saw *Rashomon* and *Metropolis* and lots of French, Russian, Czech, Japanese and other films. Being able to watch all this – the crème of world cinema – in optimal conditions was exhilarating.

You discovered jazz at the same time. How did that happen?

Thanks to my father, who plays the guitar. The music he played and listened to, at home or in the car, became part of my daily life. But contrary to what you might think, I didn't fall in love with jazz right away. I was more drawn to rock 'n' roll and blues, which my father also listened to. My interest in jazz increased gradually and really kicked in when I started in ninth grade at Princeton High School, which was less known for its sports teams than for the excellent jazz programme that had made its reputation, largely thanks to Anthony J. Biancosino, an Italian-American saxophonist, conductor and teacher who founded the Studio Band.[3] He revamped the school's music programme and thanks to him it became something really spectacular. There was a very tough, competitive atmosphere. Anyone at Princeton High with serious musical aspirations tried out for it.

A few years earlier, when I was ten or eleven, one of my cousins started playing the drums. I really loved the sound, so I copied him and started playing drums myself. By the time I got to Princeton, I had been playing for several years. I had heard about Biancosino's jazz programme, but it felt too intense because, at that time, music was more of a pastime than a serious pursuit for me. I was a bit casual, as one can be in high school, but Biancosino took an interest in me, to the extent that he pulled me out of the music ensemble I was part of and put me in the Studio Band. I suddenly found myself surrounded by people who took music far more seriously than I did. For a while, I tried to keep up by pretending that I could read music or had certain skills that I was very much lacking. Every day when I got home from school, I locked myself in my room for a kind of intensive and accelerated self-training. I forced myself to learn all the technical terms I didn't know and how to read music, and practiced the traditional drum grip.[4] I started raiding my father's jazz record collection to try and identify the most important drummers: Art Blakey, Jo Jones, Max Roach, Buddy Rich, Gene Krupa, Elvin Jones, Chick Webb, Sid Catlett. I knew their names but had never really listened to them. I also tried to get hold of videos of performances by drummers, which I watched carefully so I could copy them. I served as an accompanying musician for the Studio Band, but I really wasn't sure if I was up to becoming a lead drummer once I graduated.

Jazz – and more specifically drumming – eventually became an all-consuming passion. With friends from the Studio Band, we formed small combos and would sometimes go to New York on weekends to play on street corners or in the subway to earn some money. Four of us even had a group that performed in restaurants and at various events in the Princeton area. I went to jam sessions to listen and watch seasoned drummers, and when I got home, really inspired, I doubled the time I spent practising. I spent summers at jazz workshops and took lessons with different instructors to perfect my technique. Until I left Princeton High School in 2003, it's no exaggeration to say that jazz took up one hundred percent of my free time.

It sounds like you don't have much nostalgia for that period.

No, because from the moment I joined the Studio Band, I put cinema on hold, even though it had always been much more important to me than music. I still occasionally went to see films and talked about them with friends, and even thought about ideas for screenplays, but my obsession with cinema took a back seat. Biancosino's influence was such that music drowned out everything else, and I began to be gripped by fear: fear of humiliation, fear of being judged an impostor, fear of being excluded from the group of musicians in the Studio Band. I dramatised this chapter of my life – the vicious circle – in *Whiplash*.

We'll come back to that. The year 2003 was a kind of crossroads in your journey. You graduated from Princeton High School and entered Harvard University to study not music but cinema. You ultimately chose your original vocation. Was that a tough decision to make?

There was a kind of obviousness to it. Even during my most intense musical period, I always thought that someday I would end up making films. At the end of high school, the idea of enrolling in a music school to become a professional drummer did cross my mind, but even though I had proven to myself that I could significantly improve with practice, I had to face facts: I would never be good enough. Maybe I realised that deep down I didn't love it enough, that I wasn't ready to fully live the life of a musician.

Your roommate at Harvard was Justin Hurwitz, who later became the composer for your feature films. How did you two meet?

Justin was a freshman in the music department, and at the same time was looking for musicians for the rock band he was forming called Chester French. Since I hadn't completely given up on music yet, I joined as a drummer. At first we played for fun, but things began getting more serious, and eventually, after about a year, I decided to focus on my film studies, and the band, which originally had five members, transformed into a duo formed by D.A. Wallach, the singer, and Maxwell Drummey, the guitarist.[5]

What did you get out of your time at Harvard?

To be honest, I was initially convinced that a good level of general culture and a few specialised books would be enough to make me a filmmaker. My concentration was Visual and Environmental Studies,[6] which focused primarily on documentaries and avant-garde films – very different from the kind of films I dreamed of making. My film culture back then was limited to narrative fiction feature films and filmmakers like Hitchcock, Wilder, Truffaut and Kubrick. The first-year seminar I chose was entitled "Forms of the Non-Fiction Film." Confident in the extent of my cinephilia, I thought I knew more about the subject than any other freshman student, but when I went through the syllabus, I was astounded. I didn't know any of the films on the list, or any of their directors. That list included *Nanook of the North*, *Blood of the Beasts*, *Chronicle of a Summer*, experimental films by Stan Brakhage, Fernando Solanas' *The Hour of the Furnaces*, *Salesman* by the Maysles Brothers, *High School* and *Hospital* by Frederick Wiseman, Peter Hutton's *New York Portraits* and Chris Marker's *Sans Soleil*. They were all screened in 16 or 35mm prints, and we discussed them with the professors. It was a game-changer for me. It completely broadened my horizons, and I realised that my understanding of movies barely scratched the surface. I continued to watch avant-garde films at the Harvard Film Archive, like *La Région Centrale* by Michael Snow. Theory was complemented by practice. I learned about avant-garde production techniques, shot experimental short films on 16mm, made a kind of film diary and a small montage project that linked Jean-Luc Godard's *Band of Outsiders* to Elia Kazan's *On the Waterfront*. I was inspired by Joseph Cornell's *Rose Hobart,* which is crafted from a B-movie – George Melford's *East of Borneo* – as a love letter to the lead actress and embellished with additional music.

You completed your studies at Harvard by making your first feature film, Guy and Madeline on a Park Bench, *which you also wrote and co-edited. The film, set in Boston, follows the intertwined paths of Guy, a jazz trumpet player, played by Jason Palmer, and student Madeline, Desiree Garcia, who have a brief romantic relationship before going their separate ways. Jazz isn't the central focus of the film, but it's not relegated to the background either. The fairly conventional narrative serves as a pretext to showcase musicians individually and collectively in rehearsal, while recording, and when improvising. Was it important to incorporate jazz into your debut film?*

I think I started making films to experience music vicariously, filming musicians better than me, with whom

I could collaborate – people like Jason Palmer.[7] There are more music schools in Boston than anywhere else in the world, including Berklee College of Music and the New England Conservatory of Music, not to mention the city's numerous universities, each with its specific music programme, and historic jazz clubs like Wallie's Cafe Jazz Club.[8] Music students in Boston regularly participated in open jam sessions there. One evening I went to see a drummer I was considering for the lead role in *Guy and Madeline*, and saw Jason Palmer play the trumpet. I fell in love with his music and his powerful stage presence, so I offered him the role. I had reached a point where cinema and music had converged and were feeding each other. But I understood that my place wasn't behind a drum kit. It was behind a camera.

Guy and Madeline *bears the imprint of John Cassavetes'* Shadows. *Besides the fact that both stories are infused with jazz and featuring African American characters, the two films share aesthetic similarities. Like Cassavetes, you film the actors up close, as if the camera were brushing against their bodies, sometimes filling the entire frame with their faces.[9] This helps abstract them from the background and showcases the full range of their emotions.*

That's very true. I was also influenced by several music documentaries I watched while searching for interesting ways of shooting my own films, like *Jazz Dance* by Roger Tilton and Richard Leacock, which was a real revelation for me, *Thelonious Monk: Straight, No Chaser* by Charlotte Zwerin, and *Gimme Shelter*, which I first saw at the Film Archive. All these films were shot with the same camera, a CP-16mm, which I learned to use when I was a student. So I synthesised the music I loved with the filming techniques I had acquired, ultimately combining them with the style of Golden Age Hollywood musicals.

The opening shot of Guy and Madeline *cites two of your major sources of inspiration: Stanley Donen and Gene*

Kelly's Singin' in the Rain *and Jacques Demy's* The Umbrellas of Cherbourg. *When did you first discover Demy's film?*

Shortly after arriving at Harvard. It was a pivotal experience because I had preconceived ideas about musicals. I didn't think they could convey the kind of profound emotions that more realistic films did. To put it simply, musicals seemed the antithesis of documentary. But my discovery of Demy's film shook my convictions. At first, I felt detached from the story, even a bit annoyed by the style, because everything I disliked about musicals was exaggerated. The entire film is sung, after all.[10] And yet, gradually, the barriers that separated me from the film began to fall, one by one, so much so that in the end, I had been transported by some new emotion. It's hard to express it in words because it's so rich and complex, somewhere between tragedy and happiness – the kind of thing I had already felt when watching Ozu's films. What struck me about *The Umbrellas of Cherbourg* was Demy's ability to evoke a similar emotion within the context of a musical where everything – from the sets to the costumes to the dialogue – is artificial. Unlike Hollywood musicals, the artifice isn't hidden in Demy's work. It permeates every single frame, and yet doesn't prevent you from feeling subtle emotions. I realised that artifice and reality could not only coexist but also merge to create something unique. It's not a simple addition of the two, but something additional, which could be summarised by the formula "one plus one equals three."

Were you aware that Demy's legacy endures in French cinema? I'm thinking of films like On connaît la chanson *by Alain Resnais,* Jeanne et le garçon formidable *by Olivier Ducastel and Jacques Martineau,* 8 femmes *by François Ozon and* Les Chansons d'amour *by Christophe Honoré.*

I certainly noticed that the original musical is still very influential in France, but I'm not sure if this is solely because of Demy. All the great *auteurs* of French cinema experimented with musicals at some point: Jean-Luc Godard, Alain Resnais, Chantal Akerman, even Jacques Rivette, whose *Haut bas fragile* is my favourite French musical. It's very different in America, where after the 1970s if a musical was made, it was usually an adaptation of a Broadway show and had nothing to do with the old school musicals, which were characterised by lightness and grace. I wanted to resurrect that lost tradition.

I briefly mentioned the synopsis of Guy and Madeline, *but would like to return to the structure of the film, which is rich in narrative ideas. The opening credits, a sort of film within the film, summarise every stage of the romantic relationship between the two main characters, from their meeting to their break-up. After a flashback reveals the reasons for their separation – Guy meeting another young woman, Elena, on the subway – the story returns to the present and focuses on the new relationships the two characters have formed, before a final, almost dialogue-free and deeply moving reunion sequence. Did the structure of the screenplay come to you immediately or was it the result of trial and error?*

I explored several avenues before arriving at the final result. The script was influenced by certain films: *The Umbrellas of Cherbourg*, then *Shadows* – which I discovered shortly before shooting *Guy and Madeline* – Agnès Varda's *Cléo from 5 to 7*, the early films of Godard, like *A Woman is a Woman* and *Vivre sa vie,* and Richard Linklater's *Before Sunset*. Around the same time, I rediscovered a good number of Chaplin's films. It was a very stimulating period, during which my tastes were still very malleable. Godard, Cassavetes and Chaplin were vying for the title of "greatest director of all time" in my personal pantheon.

I also delved deeper into the world of Hollywood musicals from the 1930s, '40s and '50s, and became passionate about the ones that had fallen into obscurity, like Mamoulian's *Love Me Tonight*, with Maurice Chevalier, Milestone's *Hallelujah, I'm a Bum*, with Al Jolson, and

Minnelli's *Cabin in the Sky*, as well as two films by Stanley Donen that are very dear to my heart: *Seven Brides for Seven Brothers* and *It's Always Fair Weather*, a slightly disillusioned follow-up to *On the Town*, co-directed with Gene Kelly. These films, sometimes echoing each other, stimulated my creativity and led me to attempt all sorts of possible narrative combinations for *Guy and Madeline*. I particularly fantasised about moving from black-and-white to colour, like in Spike Lee's *She's Gotta Have It*, except I also wanted to widen the screen from the square format to CinemaScope. Several versions of the screenplay concluded with a fantastical ballet, imagined in the style of dream sequences from Minnelli's *An American in Paris* and *The Band Wagon*. I had to drop these ideas for financial reasons, of course not knowing that later I would be able to explore them in *La La Land*.

The *Guy and Madeline* screenplay eventually turned into a more conventional love story between a boy and a girl, which I wanted to film in a documentary style. I noticed that most films made by film students were weighed down by the performances of inexperienced actors. I wondered how to solve this problem, and came to the conclusion that the way to do it was to cast non-professionals and ask them to perform as if they were playing themselves. This also helped solve budget problems, because I couldn't afford professional actors, costume designers or lighting technicians, so I thought: let's make this film like an observational documentary, in the style of Wiseman – except, of course, everything would be fake.

It feels as if some sequences are entirely improvised, for example Elena's first appearance, watching a juggler in the street.

It's a good example of how we worked. We couldn't fill the streets with extras and control the movement of pedestrians, so we followed the actress – Sandha Khin, the only professional in the entire cast – with a handheld camera. At one point she stopped to watch a juggler perform. She thought he was cute, so she asked me if she could go talk to him, and I agreed… on the condition that we would keep the camera rolling. [*laughs*] She offered to go for coffee, they exchanged numbers, and when he asked for her name, she spontaneously said "Sandha," before realising that the camera was still rolling and she had to stay in character! She quickly corrected herself and said "Elena." I kept that moment in the edit because it shows the blurring of boundaries between the performers and the characters they embody. We changed their names, but they're very close to who they are in real life.

In certain parts of the film, we're in the realm of pure non-fiction. During shooting, Jason Palmer informed us that his family would be visiting, and I decided to use that by adding dialogue in the shower scene where Guy tells Elena about his family's arrival, then integrating shots into the edit where we see Jason teaching his mother to play the piano and chatting with his brother. They were talking about real things, but I would interrupt and ask them to emphasise one thing or clarify another, all for the sake of the film's narrative. Even the "pure" fiction sequences – like the meeting between Guy and Elena in the subway – include elements of reality because we were filming in a train full of real people. When we were filming the next sequence, in the bedroom, Sandha's phone rang and she answered and had a brief conversation with someone who didn't know we were filming. I put that moment in the film because it introduces a kind of romantic tension and highlights Guy's jealousy. At that time, I was interested in mixing reality and fiction, something that fascinated me in the work of Abbas Kiarostami, John Cassavetes and Maurice Pialat,[11] who all served as theoretical reference points.

From what you're saying, it seems the script must have undergone considerable changes during filming.

We followed a narrative framework, but I didn't really have a shooting script, just a synopsis, with mentions of dances and songs. I never gave a copy to the actors.

Did you ask the musicians to watch any films to prepare?

No, because I didn't want them to "act" like real actors. In our conversations, though, we did talk about cinema. I remember discussing Bertrand Tavernier's *'Round Midnight* with Jason Palmer, particularly Dexter Gordon's character. But these were informal discussions, similar to those we might have had about jazz. I never asked him to watch anything to prepare for his role.

There seem to be connections between your filming methods and jazz. While the production of Guy and Madeline *sometimes resembled collective improvisation, it seems to me less like free jazz and more like a form of "controlled freedom,"[12] to borrow an expression from the musicians of Miles Davis' second quintet.*

I wasn't initially aware of this, but did come to realise it when we were filming. The aesthetic of *Guy and Madeline* is primarily a consequence of the pitfalls I was trying to avoid. Before Harvard, my idols were Hitchcock and Welles, and I was convinced that every line of dialogue had to be written, every shot planned, the entire film visualised in my head before shooting. But when I started work on *Guy and Madeline*, I had to adapt. I needed to find a style that could spare me from glaring failure, which would undoubtedly have been the case if I had made the film like a Hollywood director, but with the limited resources and expertise of a student. Since, roughly speaking, Hollywood films have a ratio of 95 percent fiction to 5 percent reality, I decided to reverse that by injecting a small percentage of fiction into reality. This philosophy of film, which was radically new to me, was inspired by Cassavetes, Rouch and Wiseman, as well as the remarkable work of Shirley Clarke, and I became a fanatic of this style of filmmaking, to the extent that at a certain point I ditched my old references. Cinephilia or, more broadly, aesthetic taste, is like a cyclical process that inevitably moves from adulation to rejection. I went through it myself, and after

I finished at Harvard rejected the Hollywood canon and swore allegiance to cinéma vérité. And then, as I got older, I came to see that there's no need to choose between one or the other. You can love them both simultaneously and connect them together. That's the magic of cinema.

It's like Deleuze and Guattari's idea of the rhizome. Your cinephilia is expansive and interlinked. You aren't interested in building a hierarchy, but at the same time you embrace the "principle of connection and heterogeneity."[13] You're making connections between very different styles in Guy and Madeline, *sometimes even those at complete odds with each other.*

I can see references to Cassavetes, Rouch, Demy and Godard in *Guy and Madeline*. During editing, for example, I felt I should experiment more with narrative, so I incorporated bits from other films, paintings and comics, and ended up with a schizophrenic cut that felt like something out of a Godard film. I eventually abandoned that idea. Chaplin's *City Lights* was also a significant inspiration for *Guy and Madeline*: love in the city, paramours crossing paths, a kind of melancholic romance that hovers over the entire film. Everyone at Harvard loved Chaplin but said they found him too sentimental, and insisted that Buster Keaton was much better. That's when I discovered Keaton's films, like *College* and *Sherlock Jr.*, which are absolutely brilliant. I decided to take another look at Chaplin. I had seen his films as a kid, but hadn't formed an emotional connection. They seemed funny and entertaining. But rediscovering *City Lights* was a revelation. It felt like I was watching it for the first time. The final sequence, which echoes in every one of my films, is without a doubt the most beautiful moment in film history. If aliens came to Earth and asked me to explain cinema, I would show them that scene. It's the most exquisite definition of the form that exists.

That's good to hear because I feel the same way. I must have seen City Lights *at least ten times, but the intense emotion I felt the first time is still there for me. I also admire Chaplin's ability to appeal to a wide audience without turning his back on his experimental urges. Chaplin's character had an unparalleled impact on the avant-garde,[14] as did Keaton, who was adored by the Surrealists.*

I'm glad you bring that up, because I'm interested in the relationship between the avant-garde and films made for mass audiences. Chaplin and Keaton were Hollywood filmmakers, yet they clearly had avant-garde sensibilities, which is what interests me about American musicals: their ability to reach audiences while at the same time experimenting. You can reverse the question by studying the trajectory of filmmakers who started in avant-garde cinema before going to work in Hollywood. I've never understood why Dudley Murphy, one of my idols, is so unknown in the United States, despite being at the forefront of avant-garde cinema in Europe. He co-directed *Ballet Mécanique* [1924] with Fernand Léger, and later directed extraordinary musical shorts like *St. Louis Blues* [1928] and *Black and Tan Fantasy* [1929], as well as Hollywood features like *The Emperor Jones* [1933], starring Paul Robeson. His Hollywood films are also somewhat experimental. You can sense how hard he's trying to avoid the conventions of traditional fiction and limitations of the script. The films are strange, with avant-garde impulses interacting with popular cinema within the framework of the musical. Perhaps that's a unique trait of musicals, which might be the only genre capable of merging popular entertainment with the avant-garde. We see it in Minnelli's films, and even in England, in Powell and Pressburger's films. I've always thought that the musical was the Trojan horse of the avant-garde.

In Guy and Madeline, *there's a long dance sequence and tap dance numbers which, because of the small budget you were working with, are reminiscent of the famous Madison café dance in Jean-Luc Godard's* Band of Outsiders. *How did you prepare the actors?*

We rehearsed extensively with a choreographer, Kelly Kaleta, who I met at a tap dance club. She introduced me to Desiree Garcia, a post-doctoral student who occasionally danced at the club. I had to convince her, like all the other non-professionals, that she was capable of acting in the film.

For your first collaboration, Justin Hurwitz wrote a very jazzy score, hinting at his later contribution to La La Land. *I'm thinking of the piece that opens* Guy and Madeline, *which was actually re-worked for* La La Land. *Did you establish a particular working method?*

For a year or two, while we were still roommates, we worked on our respective projects, and then, when I began developing the idea of turning my thesis film into a kind of musical, I asked Justin if he wanted to compose the music, and he agreed. I could see his potential. He was absolutely brilliant, and interested in cinema. He introduced me to Bach, Mozart and Brahms, I introduced him to Charlie Parker, Duke Ellington and John Coltrane. We talked about film music, especially Michel Legrand, and I encouraged him to watch *The Umbrellas of Cherbourg* and *The Young Girls of Rochefort*, which he loved. The musical style of these two films became a direct inspiration for *Guy and Madeline*. Justin began on the piano, searching for melodies we liked, then composed the music and songs. Then I wrote the lyrics.[15] We followed the same process for *La La Land*, except that I wrote temporary lyrics for the songs, and later we collaborated with professional lyricists.

Among the songs in Guy and Madeline, *"Je savais pas," with French lyrics, pays a double homage to Godard and Legrand. It's performed by your father Bernard, who has a small role as an old crooner whom Madeline meets in New York and starts a relationship with. It's a very simple song, with catchy piano music and a few deliberate off-key notes highlighting the character's poetic clumsiness. It's fresh, touching and funny. [Damien laughs, and a warm smile lights up his face] Once the film was finished, did you have to submit it for a grade?*

No, because I left university earlier than expected. The people who worked with me on the film – Justin Hurwitz, my producer Jasmine McGlade,[16] and Adam Parker, who were my classmates – graduated in 2007 and moved to Los Angeles. I followed them to finish the film there and didn't return to Harvard except for the graduation ceremony. My thesis advisor, Robb Moss,[17] was very supportive, and I continued showing him excerpts from the film for feedback. Once the editing was done, he advised me on which festivals to submit it to. Sundance didn't want it, but the Tribeca Film Festival in New York screened it and it was sold to a distributor. I introduced the film at Tribeca, which was the start of a year-long festival tour.

Critical reception was excellent, including the Special Jury Prize at the Turin Film Festival. Guy and Madeline on a Park Bench *was even cited among the thirty best films of 2009 by* The New York Times *and* The Boston Globe.

I owe a great deal to Gerald Peary,[18] a renowned teacher and critic, who saw it before anyone else, even before it screened at Tribeca. Peary had discovered the American filmmaker Andrew Bujalski,[19] one of my sources of inspiration for *Guy and Madeline*. I already knew Bujalski – during post-production on *Guy and Madeline*, we spent a day together in Boston watching the rushes of *Beeswax*, the feature he was working on. I took the opportunity to show him excerpts from my own film, and he gave some very encouraging feedback, then advised me to send it on his behalf to Gerald Peary, who liked it enough to pass it on to Amy Taubin. She published the first critique of *Guy and Madeline* in *Film Comment*,[20] and her enthusiasm likely convinced some of her New York colleagues to go see it. We got good reviews in *Variety* and *The Village Voice*, among others.

To my knowledge, Guy and Madeline on a Park Bench *has never been released in France, and to this day there's no French DVD edition of the film. It's surprising that no distributor showed any interest, especially after the success of* La La Land, *and considering it's the foundation of your work, where so many interesting elements have yet to align.*

It's a shame, yes. A year after the screening at the Tribeca Festival, the film got a limited national release in the United States, followed by a video released by The Cinema Guild. We tried to sell it internationally but didn't have any luck. Things changed after the successes of *Whiplash* and *La La Land*, but negotiations were interrupted due to a rights issue. And we didn't have the budget to do an HD transfer from the 16mm negative. I still hope that the film might have a second life and the honour of being broadcast in France.

---

1. Pier Paolo Pasolini, preface to Jean Duflot, *Entretiens avec Pier Paolo Pasolini* (Éditions Pierre Belfond, 1970), 7.
2. Martin is one of the boys in the bottle factory in *David Copperfield* (George Cukor, 1935) and also appears in *Tom Brown's School Days* (Robert Stevenson, 1940). His younger brother, William, played one of Bob Cratchit's children in *A Christmas Carol* (Edwin L. Marin, 1938).
3. The band won first place at the Berklee Jazz Festival in Boston on five occasions, and in 2000 it secured the top spot in a national competition held at Johns Hopkins University.
4. This technique involves the drummer holding the drumstick in the palm of the hand, between the thumb and index finger, with the palm facing upward. It is favoured by jazz drummers because it allows for more nuance than the match grip, commonly used in rock music.
5. Pharrell Williams signed the group to his label, Star Trak, in 2009, the same year that Chester French's debut album, *Love the Future*, was released.
6. Later renamed the Department of Art, Film, and Visual Studies (AFVS).
7. Trumpet player and composer, recipient of numerous awards, Jason Palmer (b. 1979) has played with Herbie Hancock, Wynton Marsalis, Jeff Ballard, and Lee Konitz. He has recorded many solo albums and a double live album, *At Wally's* (2018). He is an assistant professor at Berklee College of Music.
8. Founded in 1947 by Joseph L. Walcott (alias Wally), the first African American to own a night club.
9. Regarding the importance of jazz in *Shadows*, see Gilles Mouëllic, *Jazz et cinéma* (Cahiers du cinéma, 2000).

10. Demy defines this style as follows: "A kind of opera [...] where all the words would be audible, without ever forcing the lyricism of the voices [...], sort of as if opera had followed the evolution of jazz." Quoted in Camille Taboulay, *Le Cinéma enchanté de Jacques Demy* (Cahiers du cinéma, 1996), 19.
11. Chazelle wrote a penetrating analysis of Maurice Pialat's *À nos amours* for the Criterion Collection.
12. Franck Bergerot, *Le Jazz dans tous ses états* (Larousse, 2011), 175.
13. Gilles Deleuze and Félix Guattari, *Capitalisme et schizophrénie 2: Mille plateaux* (Les Éditions de Minuit, 1980).
14. See Claire Lebossé (ed.), *Charlie Chaplin dans l'oeil des avant-gardes* (Musée d'arts de Nantes/Snoeck, 2019).
15. The lyrics of the songs from *Guy and Madeline on a Park Bench* are reproduced at the end of this book.
16. Former fencer Jasmine McGlade played a role in the development and production of *Whiplash* and was an executive producer on *La La Land*. She was married to Damien Chazelle from 2010 to 2014.
17. In addition to his academic career, Robb Moss has directed several documentary films, including *Riverdogs* (1978), *The Tourist* (1991), *The Same River Twice* (2004), and *Containment* (co-directed with Peter Galison, 2015).
18. Born in 1944, Gerald Peary taught journalism at Suffolk University (Boston) for thirty years. He has published articles on cinema in numerous newspapers (*Boston Globe*, *Los Angeles Times*, etc.) and specialised magazines (*Positif*, *Film Comment*, *Sight and Sound*, etc.), and co-edited several anthologies of interviews with directors (John Ford, Samuel Fuller, Quentin Tarantino). He has also directed documentary films and made an appearance in Andrew Bujalski's *Computer Chess* (2013).
19. Born in 1977 in Boston, Andrew Bujalski studied film in the Department of Visual and Environmental Studies at Harvard, where Chantal Akerman was his thesis advisor. He is associated with the Mumblecore movement, a strand of American independent cinema characterised by low-budget productions, the use of non-professional actors, and a significant amount of improvisation. His debut feature, *Funny Ha Ha* (2002), has been compared to the work of John Cassavetes.
20. "First Look: Alone Together. Fred and Ginger meet John Cassavetes in *Guy and Madeline on a Park Bench*," *Film Comment*, March/April 2009.

FINDING THE RIGHT TEMPO
On various screenplays

We talked about the development of your cinephilia throughout your adolescence and university years. If someone asked you to make a list of ten great films, what would they be?

Are you asking for the ten films I consider the most important, or my ten favourite films?

The ten films that have influenced you the most as a filmmaker, which might also be among your favourites.

The Umbrellas of Cherbourg instantly comes to mind. That's an easy one. And *Chronicle of a Summer*. [*Long silence.*] Dreyer's *The Passion of Joan of Arc*, *City Lights*, a short film by Bruce Baillie called *All My Life*, which is very simple but I think is an absolutely perfect film. [*He reflects again – silence.*] I would add *Blood of the Beasts* by Georges Franju, Hitchcock's *Vertigo*, Godard's *Vivre sa vie*, Welles' *Citizen Kane* and Kubrick's *Barry Lyndon*. Those are the ten films that come to mind when you ask the question – but it's constantly evolving. I forgot Renoir's *A Day in the Country.* And, of course, a film by Dudley Murphy definitely has to be on this list.

In that case, the list should have twenty names. I expected you to mention Singin' in the Rain, *which you have said is probably the greatest film of all time. Like* Babylon, *its story takes place during the transition from silent to talking cinema.*

I was interested in that period independently of *Singin' in the Rain*. I thought about including some references to it while I was writing the *Babylon* script. We'll talk about that after you've seen the film.

I'm looking forward to it. All the films you mentioned as favourites are from before the 1980s. Are there any recent ones that stand out?

I can mention a few, but it doesn't necessarily mean I have a particularly close connection with the directors who made them. Overall, I like all of Pialat's films, as well as Kieslowski's, especially *The Decalogue* and *The Double Life of Veronique*. From the 1990s, I like Kiarostami's *Close-Up*, Carax's *Les Amants du Pont-Neuf, Titanic*, and Claire Denis' *Beau Travail*. In the past twenty years, I've been impressed by Laurent Cantet's *Time Out, There Will Be Blood, The Social Network* and *Blue Is the Warmest Colour.*

Are you interested in James Gray's work?

Absolutely, yes. *The Yards* and *Two Lovers* are masterpieces. I also like Terrence Malick's films: *The Thin Red Line, The New World* and *The Tree of Life*, and some of the Coen Brothers' work, especially *Fargo* and *Inside Llewyn Davis*. Also films by Wong Kar-wai and Tsai Ming-liang.

Let's go back to your work, if you don't mind. Except for First Man, *you've written the screenplays for all your films.*

Whom do you show them to first?

A small circle of friends, including my composer Justin Hurwitz and my wife, Olivia Hamilton, who is also my producer. Then I give a draft to other producers. When pre-production is about to begin, I'll share it with key crew members like my editor Tom Cross and cinematographer Linus Sandgren.

La La Land *was supposed to be your second feature. You pitched the script to several studios but discussions went nowhere and you shelved the project rather than compromise.*

Actually, initially, it wasn't *La La Land*...

What do you mean?

I need to go back a bit. Despite some critical buzz, Hollywood expressed no interest in *Guy and Madeline on a Park Bench*, although it did catch the eye of two producers: Gary Ungar, who became my manager, and Matthew Plouffe, an executive at Focus Features. After seeing it at Tribeca, Matthew emailed and suggested we meet. That's how our professional relationship started, and I began sending him scripts. I got very excited because I hoped he and Gary could get a script I had written to James Schamus and he would produce it. I thought it was going to be my big break. I remember one screenplay in particular, a noir-style story, the kind of thing Jean-Pierre Melville or Jacques Becker would make. Matthew gave me regular feedback, but nothing happened, until one day, a bit fed up, I said, "Listen – I want Focus Features to produce one of my projects, but they haven't been interested in anything I've sent them. What's going on?" He said, "You won't win over any producers with those gangster scripts because you've never directed one. How about trying a musical instead?" According to him, financiers would then take my ideas more seriously since I had already made a musical that had received good reviews.

So I embarked on a writing spree, quickly churning out several scripts – which Matthew didn't like very much. [*laughs*] They had two things in common: a sequence with two characters dancing in a planetarium and flying into the air, and a sad ending. Besides those two things, which both later ended up in *La La Land*, the stories I had in mind were very different. One of the scripts was an ensemble film, where lots of characters cross paths in New Jersey, a mixture of *The Young Girls of Rochefort* and *A Midsummer Night's Dream*. Another, focused on two protagonists, was reminiscent of Ingmar Bergman's *Scenes from a Marriage*. Matthew noticed that my stories always took place in cities I knew, like Boston or New York, and he suggested I write a musical set in Los Angeles. The idea stuck. As I thought about it, I realised I could write a screenplay about people uprooted, about the feelings I experienced in Los Angeles, where I felt like a stranger, while tapping into the dreamlike, almost fairy-tale aspect of the City of Angels. I wrote a treatment that I gave to Jordan Horowitz and Fred Burger, two young producers Matthew had connected me with. Like me, they were from the East Coast, recently arrived in Los Angeles. The three of us embarked on a highly collaborative process, spanning several years, which resulted in the *La La Land* script. Jordan and Fred's contributions were crucial to the development of the story, plot and characters.

Was this after you had written the screenplay for Whiplash?

I'm not sure... I don't think so. Maybe I had already written *Whiplash*, but no one was interested in it. In any case, we spent a year refining the *La La Land* script, hoping that Focus Features would produce it. Then Matthew Plouffe, who was our main contact at the company, left and became an independent producer, and a few months later the studio said they were dropping the project. At the same time some producers got behind *Whiplash*, so I put *La La Land* aside and made a short film based on one sequence from *Whiplash*, in order to convince the financiers to turn it into a feature film. That paid off. Throughout this period, I was trying to raise money for *La La Land*, but no one was interested. Even after the success of *Whiplash*, studios just weren't interested in musicals. Eventually Patrick Wachsberger and Eric Feig came on board, and thanks to them Lionsgate picked it up.

In addition to your efforts to get Whiplash *and* La La Land *made, you also wrote or revised scripts that other people directed. How do you feel about them now?*

I was purely a writer for hire, without much artistic ambition. I was known for writing thrillers and single-location thrillers like *The Claim*[1] and *Grand Piano*, and soon producers were giving me treatments to develop or scripts to rewrite.

Like The Last Exorcism Part II *by Ed Gass-Donnelly, a sequel to Daniel Stamm's* The Last Exorcism. *You're credited as a co-author, even though there's absolutely nothing of what you wrote in the film. Why is that?*

Because the Writers Guild of America protects screenwriters, so when an original screenplay is revised and corrected, they prevent the name of the first author from being removed from the credits. Guild members are even more suspicious when the filmmaker himself has taken charge of the rewrite. Originally, Eli Roth had written a brief treatment, and he and Eric Newman submitted it to me to develop into a screenplay, and then they found a director who completely rewrote it. So I don't have much to do with that film, although that didn't stop me from keeping in touch with Eli and Eric, who I like a lot.

Would you ever consider directing a horror film?

Maybe, yes. I would love to make a monster movie!

10 Cloverfield Lane, the sequel to Matt Reeves' Cloverfield,[2] *which you rewrote, belongs in this category. It's formally very different from the first film, in that it doesn't use the found footage concept. Originally written by Josh Campbell and Matt Suecken and entitled* The Cellar, *it wasn't an official sequel to* Cloverfield. *Bad Robot, J.J. Abrams' company that produced the first film, took it over, and that's when you were brought in. Didn't they ask you to direct the film at one point?*

That's right. While filming the short film *Whiplash*, I worked on the script for *10 Cloverfield Lane*, which the producers liked. Just as they were about to begin production, they saw my short film and thought that *I* should be the one to direct *10 Cloverfield Lane*. It was a tempting offer, but my passion for *Whiplash* was stronger. I waited until I had financing locked up for my feature film, then stepped away from *10 Cloverfield Lane*. J.J. Abrams was very understanding when I explained why. He understood that *Whiplash* was absolutely something I really had to do. I went off and made the film, and Dan Trachtenberg took over *10 Cloverfield Lane*. He rewrote and significantly improved parts of the script. He did a good job.

It has some good moments. Besides an excellent cast, it's quite successful in blending genres. It's a post-apocalyptic science-fiction film but also a claustrophobic thriller, with one of the characters turning out to be a serial killer. Howard, played with great relish by John Goodman, talks about a possible Russian attack, and outside the bunker where he's holed up with his two guests, something strange and evil – an epidemic, perhaps – is decimating humanity. The parallels to current events are unsettling.

That's true, now that you mention it! [*laughs*]

What's your state of mind when you're in the writing phase?

It varies a lot. I might feel inspired one day and overwhelmed the next. When I've spent a lot of time writing, I start feeling impatient and eager to get back behind the camera. The opposite also happens: when I've spent a lot of time on a shoot or in editing, I feel the urge to write again.

I would like to talk a little more about your screenplay Grand Piano, *which the Spanish filmmaker and composer Eugenio Mira directed in 2013. It's a musical thriller with echoes of Alfred Hitchcock and Brian De Palma. Tom Selznick, a renowned pianist suffering from stage fright, returns after five years and gives a concert to honour his mentor, composer Patrick Godureaux, who died a year earlier. As the concert begins, Tom discovers death threats written on his sheet music. He realises he's the target of a blackmailer who is threatening to kill him and his wife Emma, a famous actress in the audience, if he plays a wrong note. Did you ever consider directing the film?*

Never.

It's easy to see it as a variation on the final concert sequence at the Albert Hall in Hitchcock's The Man Who Knew Too Much.

I set myself a kind of challenge: to expand on the epilogue of Hitchcock's film. I used the same metaphor as in *Whiplash*: when a musician goes on stage and makes the mistake of hitting a wrong note or being off-tempo, it's like risking everything. That's how I felt when I was a drummer. I thought it would be fun to translate that feeling in a very literal way by making my pianist the target of a killer. Unlike *Whiplash*, however, *Grand Piano* is a hyperbolic and nightmarish farce.

The screenplay relies on a MacGuffin: the killer wants to get hold of a key hidden in the piano mechanism, supposedly to open a safe where Godureaux's fortune is hidden. This narrative device is obviously there to generate a sense of suspense during the concert. After all, it's unlikely that a blackmailer would risk threatening a soloist in the middle of a concert hall full of people just to steal a key.

I couldn't care less about the key, of course.

Hitchcock had composer Arthur Benjamin write a cantata, The Storm Clouds, *for the 1934 version of* The Man Who Knew Too Much. *The cantata, which was arranged by Bernard Herrmann for the 1956 remake, is nearly ten minutes long and is heard in its entirety in the film. This idea is pushed even further in* Grand Piano. *Victor Reyes composed a concerto in three movements and a sonata,* La Cinquette, *known to be unplayable. It's the music that creates the suspense, as the pianist's survival depends on not hitting a wrong note. Hitchcock said that for the concert scene in* The Man Who Knew Too Much *to achieve its maximum strength, "all of the viewers should be able to read music."[3] Do you agree with that statement?*

The ideal is undoubtedly an audience of music enthusiasts, but a filmmaker has to be able to reach everyone, including people who would have no idea how to decipher a musical score. In *The Man Who Knew Too Much*, the audience is considerably assisted by the fact that the hidden shooter in the room is planning on assassinating an ambassador with a revolver at the precise moment of the only cymbal strike in the cantata. It's easy to understand by looking at the score, even if you have no knowledge of music theory. Hitchcock also managed to build incredible moments of suspense in musical sequences without using the music itself. I'm thinking of that brilliant scene in *Young and Innocent* where the hero searches for an assassin with a nervous tic. Towards the end of the film, he finds himself in a room where a jazz orchestra is playing, which the camera moves across in a single shot until zooming in on the eyes of the drummer – who has a tic. It's a great camera move. As for *Grand Piano*, I was interested in the very definition of what constitutes a wrong note. Similarly, in *Whiplash*, the suspense revolves around the notion of good or bad tempo. Andrew's tempo during rehearsal sequences is almost perfect, and yet Fletcher believes that he's either behind or ahead of the others. The idea is to explore the ambiguity of the situation. Is Fletcher a genius capable of hearing dissonances that escape ordinary mortals, or is he a manipulative pervert, as evidenced by the fact that he humiliates the trombone player and throws him out of the orchestra, even though he hadn't played a wrong note?

Fletcher as a kind of anti-Art Tatum.[4] It's an intriguing idea. I'm much less convinced by the way you handle the concept of a wrong note in your Grand Piano *script. But the main issue with Eugenio Mira's film is the conjunction between music and dialogue. Tom communicates with his assailant through an earpiece, which has the drawback of relegating the music into the background. The viewer isn't really listening to it anymore, whereas it really should be the source of suspense. The tension, suspense and emotion in the final sequence of* Whiplash *come directly from us hearing the music. From this perspective, it feels as if* Whiplash *was an opportunity for you to address* Grand Piano*'s shortcomings.*

You might be right. At the same time, the stakes in each story are so different. I came to Hollywood to write scripts and make a living. I had no choice: I would never have succeeded in that if I had continued making films like *Guy and Madeline*. I had no high artistic ambitions when I wrote *Grand Piano*. I was just following the conventions of the single-location thriller genre, which require keeping the reader or viewer engaged at every turn. With *Whiplash*, on the other hand, I was aiming for a purer kind of filmmaking, but selling a story to Hollywood that's primarily about music is challenging. It's just not very marketable. The problems you've identified in *Grand Piano* aren't Eugenio Mira's fault. I had to keep it gripping and get the audience's attention. I wrote it so that the reader would want to do only one thing: turn the page and see what happens next. Once I developed a bit of a reputation as a screenwriter, I could finally go back to more personal projects without worrying too much about the commercial side of things or the effectiveness of my scripts. But instead of throwing away everything I had learned as a screenwriter, I realised it would be exciting to blend personal stories with a writing style that really captured the reader – as powerful as a thriller or genre film. And so my experiences of *Grand Piano* were very helpful when it came to *Whiplash*. I also went to visit Eugenio Mira on the film set in Barcelona, where I spent a few days and learned a lot from how he shot the music scenes. It was very inspiring.

---

1. Listed on Hollywood's Black List of the best unproduced scripts, *The Claim* is the story of a father with a troubled past who investigates the disappearance of his daughter, while also dealing with a couple who insist that she is their child. In 2017, *Variety* reported that a production company had optioned the film, but no specific filming date was announced.
2. Shot entirely from a first-person perspective and presented in a found footage style, *Cloverfield* is about the attack on New York City by a creature from the deep sea. It was a major box-office success, grossing over $172 million, which encouraged producers to turn it into a franchise. In addition to *10 Cloverfield Lane*, a third instalment, *The Cloverfield Paradox*, directed by Julius Onah, was released in 2018.
3. Alfred Hitchcock, *Hitchcock/Truffaut* (Touchstone, 1985), 231.
4. Renowned pianist Art Tatum used to teach his students that in jazz, "there's no such thing as a wrong note."

FASTER THAN MUSIC
Whiplash

It's nearly the end of July, but despite expectations, the editing of Babylon *continues.*

We've fallen behind. In theory, we should have finished by the end of September, but it looks like we'll spill over into October. We've been editing in parallel with the shoot, which means we've been going for a year, since July 2021.

Is this new for you?

Entirely. I knew it would be a lengthy process because the film is going to be more than three hours, but I was hoping to finish it before the summer. Fortunately, it has no impact on the film's release, which is scheduled for December in the United States. We still have some wiggle room. Some things need to be fine-tuned, and Justin Hurwitz is putting the finishing touches on the music mix.

Babylon *marks your fifth collaboration in as many films. You're walking in the footsteps of legendary filmmaker-composer duos, where images and melodies are inseparable. Just try thinking of Federico Fellini, Sergio Leone, Jacques Demy and Steven Spielberg without thinking of Nino Rota, Ennio Morricone, Michel Legrand and John Williams. Do you consider Justin Hurwitz your alter ego?*

You could say that. We go way back, all the way to college. I trust him absolutely, and consider him a co-creator.

Writing the score for a film usually begins at a more or less advanced stage of the process, but in your case it starts very early, right from the screenplay stage, even before pre-production has begun.

That's right. Justin starts composing without any visuals as guidance, based solely on the script – the descriptions and cues – that I've written.

He's a true tunesmith. It reflects your own sensitivity to music.

I love films where the music is a "character" in its own right. French and Italian films from the 1950s and 1960s were my first source of inspiration. Besides the Fellini-Rota and Demy-Legrand collaborations, I really like the music composed by Antoine Duhamel, Georges Delerue and Martial Solal for Godard's films, and Jean Constantin's music orchestrated by Michel Legrand for Truffaut's *The 400 Blows*. Overall, I prefer original soundtracks structured around melodies, which hasn't been the norm in Hollywood since the 1990s, where these days there's a preference for soundscapes and ambient music. The figure of a composer writing actual melodies isn't very common in filmmaking today.

Unlike your other films, there isn't a standout musical theme in Whiplash. *Besides Justin Hurwitz and Tim Simonec's pieces,[1] the soundtrack features several jazz standards, the most famous being "Caravan," composed in 1936 by Juan Tizol and arranged by Duke Ellington. The title of the film is borrowed from a piece by Hank Levy. Did you choose it because of its symbolic meaning?*

It's much simpler than that: it's the first piece we played on the first day I joined the Studio Band. I couldn't read music very well, and found myself in front of a score in a seven-beat measure. Until then I had only played pieces in three or four beats. I was sitting behind the drummer, trying to follow the rhythm, but the piece seemed very complex and I was completely lost. Luckily for me, unlike what happens to Andrew Neiman in the film, they didn't put me on drums on day one.

The screenplay for Whiplash *is partly inspired by your experience as a drummer. Young Andrew Neiman dreams of joining Terence Fletcher's orchestra at the Shaffer Conservatory in New York. When he succeeds, he gets caught in an unhealthy spiral, with his teacher using unorthodox methods to push him beyond his limits. Is* Whiplash *semi-autobiographical fiction?*

My teenage experiences were the basis of my inspiration for the story, but I wouldn't consider *Whiplash* a semi-autobiographical or biographical film. It's a completely invented narrative based on autobiographical elements. I'm not Andrew, and Fletcher is a long way from Biancosino. It was more about translating the feelings my teacher evoked in me, projecting them onto the screen to share them with the audience. Some parts of the film are based on reality, but most of it is rearranged, exaggerated, or completely made up.

Johnny Simmons played the role of Andrew Neiman in the short film. Why was he replaced by Miles Teller in the feature film?

From the start, even before shooting the short film, I had my eye on Miles Teller. I had seen him in John Cameron Mitchell's *Rabbit Hole*, which he was so good in. He had an authenticity and maturity that's very rare among actors his age, especially when playing high school or college students. His name quickly jumped to the top of the list of actors I was considering for the role of Andrew Neiman. But, as I explained, things didn't go as planned. We were unable to finance the feature film initially, so on the producers' advice I made a short film from one of the scenes in the script. Jason Reitman, our executive producer, regularly cast J.K. Simmons in his films, and through him we managed to convince J.K. to play Fletcher. It was a sort of gamble: if we could secure funds to produce the feature film, he would reprise his character. Things were less obvious for the role of Andrew. We held auditions and our casting director suggested giving it to Johnny Simmons, who is an excellent actor. A year later, as we prepared for the feature shoot, we knew we needed an actor capable of taking Andrew as far as he goes in the second part of the script. Miles provided the necessary assurances because he had a natural robustness, tinged with a kind of vulnerability. I was sure he could portray the full range of the character's emotions. When we started working together, I discovered that Miles was very different from his character in *Rabbit Hole*. He's actually quite self-assured, humorous, extroverted – completely the opposite of Andrew in the early sequences of *Whiplash*. The trajectory that the character reaches at the end of the film is closer to the "real" Miles Teller.

One thing you considered when choosing the actors was their knowledge of music. J.K. Simmons has a background as a music teacher, and Miles Teller has been playing drums since he was fifteen.

The main actors all had musical backgrounds. Miles had practiced a lot on the drums and knew how to handle himself in front of a drum kit. As for J.K., he knew how to conduct an orchestra, something I didn't initially know when I handed him the script. Nate Lang, who played one of the rival drummers, was a real musician and even became Miles' part-time coach during pre-production. He was in his comfort zone, just like the extras playing the instrumentalists. Some were actors with musical backgrounds, but most were professional musicians capable of playing any jazz standard.

I gather you didn't use playback for the musical scenes.

That's right, for the simple reason that it's nearly impossible to mime playing the drums, or most instruments, for that matter. The musicians in the film weren't pretending. However, the sounds you hear weren't always produced by the actors. Sometimes they're from the live performance, and in other places it's a mix of live music and music recorded in post-production. For some sequences, we had to completely rerecord the music, which means that sometimes it's Miles Teller playing, while in other parts of the film he's "dubbed" by other drummers.

Did you use multiple cameras to shoot the music scenes?

We worked primarily with two cameras, except for the final sequence, where we had five.

How many takes did you usually do for each shot on average?

Not as many as I would have liked. When I got to the fourth or fifth, I knew I was getting into dangerous territory because time was tight. We only had nineteen days to shoot the film. It was a very different experience on the set of *Guy and Madeline*, where we took frequent breaks to shape the film at our own pace. With *Whiplash*, we were under pressure from day one, with no room for improvisation beyond the predetermined plan. For each shot I tried not to go beyond two or three takes. In general, two good takes for each shot is enough – that's the rule I usually try to stick to. For *Whiplash*, this was basically dictated by time constraints. As soon as a take seemed good to me, even if it was the first one, we moved on to the next shot, hoping there would be no issues in post-production. Each shooting day was a battle. On a typical shoot, you rarely exceed about a dozen setups a day, a number we multiplied by four for *Whiplash*.

To save as much time as possible, the film was entirely storyboarded, so I knew exactly what shots I needed. The scene at Andrew's dinner with his uncle, aunt and cousins, for example, which was the very first scene we shot, could have easily taken us three days, but we only had half a day, so we were careful to stick to the storyboards. Instead of long takes lasting several minutes, we filmed separate shots for each line of dialogue. We did the same for the music sequences: each measure or timecode corresponded to a shot. Of course, we did full takes when necessary, but most of the time we settled for shorter shots. In many ways, filming *Whiplash* was like solving a mathematical puzzle. Because we knew the film would be heavily edited, with a geometric structure and lots of sharp cuts, we had to construct very deliberate shots. It was the editing that created a sense of velocity, making the visuals as rhythmic as the music.

Since musicians are generally static when playing their instruments, it's the relationship between shots that creates rhythmic pacing. Compared to that, filming a car race, a boxing match or a battle sequence is a walk in the park. Put simply: *Whiplash* is Eisenstein's "montage of attractions" and *La La Land* is Bazin's "forbidden montage." Of course, it's vital to understand that Eisenstein's method only works if the frames are meticulously constructed. A vertical line corresponds to a perpendicular, a diagonal reflects another diagonal, circular shapes intersect, and so on. If a filmmaker prioritises editing over long continuous shots without paying particular attention to the framing, the result is inevitably poor. That's why *Battleship Potemkin* is a much better action film than most made in the last fifty years, even though the camera is static. Eisenstein uses highly graphic compositions that echo one another. This was a tremendously helpful lesson when I made *Whiplash*.

Whiplash is your first experience working with professional actors. What's your approach to directing actors? Are you very hands-on with your cast or do you like to let them experiment?

I like to see what actors bring to the table before throwing out my own ideas. When a director jumps in too early with fixed ideas, they never really get to see how the characters might have developed. I prefer having very general conversations with the actors about their roles, but during pre-production we stick mostly to the bigger picture. By the end of the first day of shooting, I have a fairly clear idea of how the actors see their characters, and we talk about it. *Whiplash* was unique in this respect because we didn't really have time for rehearsals, so when shooting began, Miles Teller and J.K. Simmons hadn't spent much time together. Due to our tight schedule, everything became about efficiency, including directing the actors. Once we got through the first few takes, I could step in to guide them, but only if it was really necessary.

J.K. Simmons' physicality is striking. His costume is limited to a black jacket, trousers and t-shirt, the simplicity of which is offset by the exaggerated facial expressions and gestures.

All credit to J.K. Simmons. I remember the email he sent me during pre-production for the short film, suggesting the idea of wearing very simple, all-black, perfectly clean clothes. He also thought that Fletcher should be in optimal physical shape, which resonated with how I wanted to portray music in the film: not as a cerebral activity or a light, enjoyable exercise but as a physical ordeal where sweat mixes with blood. The idea of characterising music physically seemed surprisingly absent from most films that have dealt with it, even though a musician's daily work is as physical as that of a high-level athlete or an infantry soldier. It has nothing to do with musical composition, which is more akin to a writer's work. J.K. crafted Fletcher with the body of a sports coach or a military instructor: shaved head, bulging muscles. I loved that idea, which was very different from what I imagined a music teacher should look like.

You mention that films about music rarely show the physical suffering of musicians, but actually this is exactly what Jacques Audiard's The Beat That My Heart Skipped, *the remake of James Toback's* Fingers, *does.*

I love that film. The emotional power of the scenes when Thomas is practising the piano is very familiar to me as a musician. The scene of the failed audition is definitely the most moving for me. Unlike *Whiplash*, the violence in Jacques Audiard's film isn't figurative – it's very real. It's a gangster film full of brutality and murder, and yet it's the failed audition that comes over as the most tragic and violent. For much of the film, the camera is constantly in motion, building up energy, but the audition is shot from only two angles, shot/reverse shot. Thomas starts playing the piano in front of Mr. Fox, messes up, starts again, messes up again, stands up, leaves the room. All the suspense of the film builds up to this sequence, which is dispatched very abruptly in two minutes. It's brutal. This moment encapsulates exactly what I constantly faced as a musician: how to surpass my limits and become *better*. I wasn't looking for a new way of expressing myself or creating some spiritual transfiguration through music, I just wanted to play well. *The Beat That My Heart Skipped* resonated with all of that. It's a long way from the romantic ideal commonly associated with the figure of the virtuoso musician. I can't say it directly influenced *Whiplash*, but it was definitely drifting through my subconscious when I was working on the film.

You met Romain Duris afterwards, didn't you?

In Paris, yes, right after the release of *Whiplash*.

What was the occasion?

We had a scheduled meeting. I wanted to exchange thoughts with him because I admired his work. It turns out he had seen and liked *Whiplash*.

You probably know that he also plays the drums?

I do. We talked about that. But I mostly remember spending the whole discussion asking him questions about *The Beat That My Heart Skipped*.

Let's go back to Fletcher, who is a kind of cousin of gunnery sergeant Hartman in Kubrick's Full Metal Jacket. *They share a colourful vocabulary, and both are full of misogynistic, anti-Semitic and homophobic slurs.*

When I first saw *Full Metal Jacket*, I was struck by the fact that it resonated with my experiences as a musician more than any film about music ever did. I recognised the emotions I had felt in the Studio Band, where there was an atmosphere like that of a training camp. When I was writing the screenplay, I imagined Fletcher to be very different physically, more like Tony Soprano than Sergeant Hartman. Remember, my teacher was Italian-American. [*laughs*] I knew that his appearance would depend on the actor who was cast, so I deliberately left out of the script details about his appearance. I focused on defining him through behaviour and dialogue. To be honest, when Jason Reitman suggested J.K. Simmons' name, I had some doubts. I had less in mind his character in the series *Oz* than the later roles he played, like Jameson in *Spider-Man* or Juno's father, in Reitman's eponymous film. I associated him more with comedic or tender roles, and wondered if he would be capable of instilling fear in an audience, since most people would have a rather sympathetic image of him. Just before shooting the short film, when J.K. asked me if I had any guidance for him, all I said was, "Don't set any limits for yourself. Nothing is too extreme for this character." I wanted him, in these explosive moments, to transform into some kind of animal, as if controlled by a superhuman force. This is exactly what he did, which paved the way for the feature.

That's similar to what Brian De Palma told Sean Penn just before they filmed Casualties of War. *A scene in* Whiplash *also reminds me of a passage from that film.*

Which one?

The one where Fletcher physically assaults Neiman by slapping him repeatedly. It feels like those blows weren't staged. In one scene in Casualties of War, *Penn repeatedly slaps John*

Leguizamo. After the thirteenth take, Leguizamo couldn't feel his jaw because Penn had been so brutal.[2]

I remember Miles telling J.K. not to hold back. We intensified the brutality of the slaps in the edit, but it's true that Miles' flushed cheeks had nothing to do with makeup. I should clarify that unlike Sean Penn, J.K. Simmons isn't a Method actor. He's what you call a working actor. When he steps onto the set, he becomes his character, but between takes he puts it aside.

Are you saying that Simmons didn't maintain the hostility between his character and Andrew when they weren't filming, unlike Sean Penn and Michael J. Fox on the set of Casualties of War*?*

It was actually the opposite. They joked around and kept the atmosphere very light. J.K. Simmons takes his job very seriously and is a complete professional who doesn't push against the boundaries that have been set for him. There was, however, a general intensity on the set because the shoot was a real race against time, and the entire crew was fuelled by a kind of nervous energy.

Does Andrew Neiman's Jewishness, as mentioned by Fletcher, hold any particular significance for you?

I found it interesting that the audience might think Andrew is Jewish. As a character, he's a bit hard to pin down precisely. He wants to become a great musician, but his family background is completely foreign to the world of music. His name is pronounced "Nayman" but everyone calls him "Neeman," which is a kind of nickname. Perhaps he's an assimilated Jew, or perhaps his appearance and name – which Fletcher uses to humiliate him – suggest he's Jewish when he isn't.

Let's talk about the opening of Whiplash.

The idea was that it's a kind of microcosm of the entire film.

The question of perspective seems crucial. It's a forward tracking shot that takes us through a corridor to the room where Andrew is practising the drums. Thanks to the reverse shot, we see that it's a subjective shot. We discover Andrew through Fletcher's eyes, which are those of the "tormentor." This prologue seems representative of the ambiguous relationship with the audience which you establish throughout the film. We certainly suffer with Andrew, but we also experience a kind of enjoyment in seeing him pushed to his limits by Fletcher and transcending himself in pain. You're confronting us with a moral dilemma.

That's an interesting hypothesis. I don't remember how conscious I was of that. [*A brief silence.*] I do think, however, that I was trying less to convey an idea to the audience than communicate sensations, tempo and rhythm – to put it in musical terms. I had this sense that the film had to be made as if Fletcher and Andrew were its authors. In other words, by embracing their way of seeing the world. Originally, the script was equally about the two characters. As with Andrew, we saw Fletcher outside school, at his home, in more personal moments. It became clear during editing that we had to focus exclusively on Andrew and discard all aspects of his teacher's private life.

Speaking of personal moments, one detail caught my eye. In Andrew's room is a poster, prominently displayed, of Buddy Rich, with one of his famous phrases: "If you don't have ability, you wind up playing in a rock band." In La La Land, *pop-rock music appears again as the antithesis of jazz, emblematic of the commercial, ignoble music that Sebastian disapproves of. And yet, although it had its defenders, that's exactly how jazz was considered by many European intellectuals in the 1930s.[3] The philosopher Theodor Adorno, for example, saw it as a symptom of "cultural decadence."[4] To what extent is the vision of music expressed by your characters a reflection of your own?*

Allow me, before responding, to clear up any ambiguity: *I love rock!!!* Joking aside, I've always been interested in how artistic forms evolve, how yesterday's avant-garde becomes today's norm, and how what was considered revolutionary eventually becomes part of the established order. This is a very general observation that extends far beyond art and applies to politics and other aspects of life. When the "marginal" evolves and becomes "dominant," it takes on a negative dimension synonymous with "compromise." When Adorno wrote his famous texts about jazz,[5] that type of music was becoming the most popular of its time. His philosophical tone would probably be quite different today, because jazz has been supplanted in the galaxy of music by rock and now rap. Musicians like Kenny Clarke, Charlie Parker and Dizzy Gillespie revolutionised jazz, which shifted from the mainstream and lost some of its popularity.

From the moment I started making music, I've had a longing for that bygone era when jazz held the same status as pop-rock or rap does today. I regularly played in a quartet with a saxophonist-clarinettist whose worst enemy was Charlie Parker. For him, the golden age of jazz began with Buddy Bolden, continued with Bix Beiderbecke and Benny Goodman, and ended with Lester Young. I was struck by how out of touch he could be – this teenager from 1990s New Jersey who had never set foot in the Kansas City of the 1930s. He had formed his own vision of jazz through his readings and the music he listened to. Fortunately, he eventually changed direction and came to love John Coltrane.

When I was younger, I kind of followed a similar path. I was convinced that drum kits made after the 1950s had somehow lost their essence. I idolised the formal aspect and sound quality of drum kits from the swing era, even the pre-swing era – the time of Baby Dodds, Chick Webb, Sid Catlett. That led me to modify how I used the snare drum. Two things indicate which "side" a drummer is on: how he holds his drumsticks – traditional grip vs. match grip – and the height of the snare drum. When I learned to play, it seemed perfectly logical that the snare drum should be angled upward, which meant holding the sticks with the timbale grip. [*He mimics the posture.*] Later, I learned that this position had evolved since the Dixieland era. A drummer like Baby Dodds, inspired by the marching bands that he trained with, played with the snare drum tilted forward. It's fascinating to see how, decade after decade, the tilt of the snare drum progressively shifted from low to high. All this is to say that it's not the best idea to become so fixated on an era, a style or technique, because forms are constantly evolving.

My teacher, Anthony Biancosino, had a pretty strict conception of music. Despite his classical orchestral training, he was obsessed with the spirit of swing orchestras, which he wanted to recreate in the Studio Band. He raved about Fletcher Henderson, Harry James, Artie Shaw, Benny Goodman and Duke Ellington. Sometimes he allowed us to play standards from the 1960s or 1970s, but if he heard someone practising Led Zeppelin, as happened one time, he would get upset and say, "Why are you wasting your time playing that nonsense?" It was fascinating, because at our age, we all thought that Led Zeppelin was the old guard! But Biancosino reacted to canonised rock as if it were Britney Spears. [*laughs*] I found it all pretty irrational, which pushed me to think about why he felt that way, and figured that it reflected the worldview of a "rebellious minority" – passionately engaged, going against the mainstream vision.

It's easy to ridicule behaviour like that, which I kind of did with Sebastian in *La La Land*, who for me is a comic character – a jazz nerd[6] – for whom music ended in 1960. In *Whiplash*, this irrationality is no longer funny or charming – it has become toxic, and leads to masochism and cynicism. But I do believe that in both films, it's also possible to celebrate this worldview for its idealism and nobility because it's evident that the motivations guiding these characters have nothing to do with money, success or awards. They have chosen the opposite path, that of resistance. It's not necessarily my way of seeing things, although there's a bit of me in each of them. I look at them from a certain distance with a mix of affection, scepticism, criticism and admiration. Still, no – I don't think music ended in 1960, and I also don't think rock is the music of the devil! [*laughs*]

When Whiplash *was released, it was far from universally praised within the jazz community. Some took it literally, seeing it as a critique of the jazz world. Richard Brody in* The New Yorker *had especially harsh words, calling it a "grotesque and ludicrous caricature."[7] He particularly reproached you for making Buddy Rich, whom he considers an overrated drummer, Andrew's idol.*

I've always found it curious that a critic would reject a work of fiction solely because one of the characters doesn't share their musical tastes. It reflects a particularly narrow view of cinema. Some critics have also lectured me, claiming that the portrayal of jazz musicians in *Whiplash* is inaccurate – despite them never having touched a musical instrument in their lives. I can't take such attacks seriously. These people have no arguments.

The choice of Buddy Rich feels significant because he is probably the drummer who best embodies a kind of alliance between technical virtuosity and masculinity, with a certain hardness in his playing. Unlike, for example, Jo Jones, who had a very airy and sunny style.

Buddy Rich was one of my instructor's idols, and he conveyed to me a message similar to the one Fletcher has for Andrew in the film, that Rich was the epitome of drumming excellence. Looking back, I understand it much better now. Buddy Rich embodies a muscular, aggressive approach to music, where technical excellence takes precedence above all else. The gap between Buddy Rich and Jo Jones is similar to the one that separates Oscar Peterson from Thelonious Monk on the piano. Monk may not be as technically virtuosic as Peterson, and yet I respond much more to his music, to the extent that I would argue he's a better musician. Of course, there's debate about the importance of technique in a performer's play, and at what point it turns a piece into an exercise in vain, empty style. In the context of the Studio Band, technique was the most important thing, or at least one of the most important. In Biancosino's eyes, technique was the very essence of jazz and sparked its own kind of emotion in people. You experience emotion when listening to Buddy Rich play. Maybe it's not the kind that resonates with you personally, and even less so with Richard Brody. It's certainly very different from what Jo Jones communicates. But it can't be denied. Beyond that, Biancosino and Buddy Rich shared a perspective on music that was tied to their personalities outside of music. Rich was known to be an extremely aggressive and demanding bandleader. The famous recordings where he insults the musicians, like Fletcher in *Whiplash*, are evidence of this. You're right to say that when you watch Rich play, that aggressiveness totally overshadows any joy or excitement, so it makes total sense why Fletcher and Andrew idolise Buddy Rich in the movie. If I had gone with Jo Jones instead, it would have been a very different film.

This also explains why Andrew is less concerned with studying the subtleties of how the great drummers play than with training to become the best and to battle his rivals. It touches on one of the criticisms made by Adorno about jazz: its close association with sport. Whiplash *adopts the iconography of boxing films. You show Andrew's injuries, the bandages on his fingers, the blood stains on the snare drum and the ice he dips his hands into to relieve the pain – shots straight out of Martin Scorsese's* Raging Bull.

That's exactly it. And in this conception of jazz, it's true that there isn't much room for the noble values of music as subtle and nuanced, the spirit of enjoyment, love and poetry. The jazz world in *Whiplash* isn't as vibrant as in reality. The film presents audiences with a small, albeit reductionist, fragment of it. But it's the one I experienced personally.

One thing that struck me when I watched the film again is that it doesn't in any way deal with modern communication technology. At no point do Fletcher's students think about exposing him by filming in class with their cell phones or posting on social media[8] – the kind of thing that has become commonplace over the last few years. It's as if there's an unspoken rule of silence in that conservatory.

Perhaps it's simply because my teacher would never have allowed his students to have a cell phone at a rehearsal. When I was in high school, we were years away from the widespread use of smartphones. By the time I filmed *Whiplash*, things had evolved, but it was only in 2017, with the Me Too movement, that everything accelerated. Fletcher's attitude, even if it sparks rumours and gossip, doesn't end up as viral content all over the Internet, which would probably happen if the story played out today.

Fletcher tells Neiman several times that when Charlie Parker was a young musician, he had a cymbal thrown at him by Jo Jones during a jam session because he was playing so badly. He claims it "nearly decapitated" him. The anecdote is true, with one detail left out: Jo Jones actually threw the cymbal at Parker's feet, not his head, to surprise and humiliate him, never intending to harm him, as Clint Eastwood depicts it in Bird. *Several critics pointed out this "mistake," but none hinted that Fletcher might be deliberately twisting the story to mess with Andrew and justify his actions, like throwing a chair at his head during rehearsal.*

This is exactly the kind of "inconsistency" that critics in the United States like to point out. Cinema has been around for over a century, yet critics still struggle to separate fiction from reality. To satisfy them, the film would almost need to come with a disclaimer stating that the ideas expressed by the characters aren't necessarily those of the filmmaker. It's akin to infantilising the audience. I prefer to laugh about it.

The values emphasised by Fletcher – hegemonic masculinity, self-improvement, elitism, survival of the fittest – led some critics to describe Whiplash *as "fascist." To a journalist who questioned you about it, you replied somewhat provocatively: "I'd rather make a good fascist film than a bad left-wing film."*[9] *You probably had in mind the historical debate that stirred French criticism about Samuel Fuller's work, when some denounced his anti-communist, even "fascist" positions, while others, like Luc Moullet, advocated watching his films primarily for their formal qualities. Hence his famous line, one that Godard later inverted: "Morality is a question of tracking shots."[10] Is that a position you share?*

Absolutely. Framing is all about morality. The moment we begin judging art based on conventional morality, whether it's political or religious, it becomes something other than art. That doesn't mean an artist has no moral responsibility, but their primary responsibility, from my point of view, should be to create a work as honest and personal as possible, based on their feelings. In the specific case of cinema, that thing we call staging makes all the difference. I've always thought that if so many people keep going to see Mozart's *Don Giovanni* at the opera, it's less because of psychological, literary or narrative considerations than for the music, even though the elements of the story enhance its emotional power. When the ghost of the Commandant appears at the end of act two and declares in a deep bass voice, "*Don Giovanni, a cenar teco…*," it's emotionally quite overwhelming, partly because of what happened earlier in the story, but mostly thanks to the incredible musical force of the piece. Music is to opera what staging is to cinema: the narrative, psychological or political aspects of a story aren't an end in themselves but a means to an end. The goal is staging. That's the basis of what I call "pure cinema."

You mentioned this idea before. What exactly do you mean by "pure cinema"?

It's a way of conveying sensations through sound and image. It's not easy to define it precisely… An abstract film by Brakhage, an animated film in the style of Disney's *Fantasia*, or a film by Eric Rohmer are, for me, examples of "pure cinema." When I watch one of Rohmer's moral tales, the actors' faces, the framing, the tension between physicality and listening, the tenderness of Nestor Almendros' cinematography all contribute to creating moments of "pure cinema," which is very different from simply reading a script written by Rohmer himself.

The notion "pure cinema" seems to be in opposition to the "impure cinema" defended by André Bazin or Serge Daney.[11] Isn't cinema – an art that encompasses all other arts – by definition "impure"?

It's true that the notion of "purity" as applied to cinema is a bit contradictory. Perhaps I'm not using the right term. All I mean is: what is it that makes cinema fundamentally different from other arts? Cinema is the combination of different elements – music, image, sound, colour, light, time and rhythm – all arranged through editing. But this combination exudes a unique visual power that you won't find anywhere else.

If I understand correctly, you're talking about taking all these mixed and "impure" elements and creating something "pure," as if the filmmaker is a kind of alchemist, who starts with mud and ends up with gold.[12]

The alchemical metaphor fits perfectly. That's exactly what I mean.

Given everything we've been talking about, I feel that your conception of cinema lies somewhere between that of Godard and De Palma. The former made Michel Subor say in Le Petit Soldat *that cinema is "the truth twenty-four times per second," while the latter claims it's actually "a lie twenty-four times per second."*

It's funny. I've always had a different take on that line from *Le Petit Soldat*. I thought it was meant to be tongue-in-cheek. How do you say that in French?

Ironique?

Yes, that's it… *ironique*. Okay, so: cinema is the truth twenty-four times per second, but within a single second, you have a thousand milliseconds, so you could argue that cinema is the truth twenty-four times per second, but also a lie a thousand times per second. That's kind of what I think, that there's inevitably some truth in the cinema of Godard, De Palma... Chazelle. [*laughs*] Every film is a documentary about its own making, full of lies. Even though digital technology changes things, a filmmaker is always limited by what the camera can capture. Bazin talked about this. It's what fundamentally sets cinema apart from other arts, like painting or literature. The most artificial shots of Hitchcock, Sirk and Minnelli have a documentary quality to them. I've always been troubled by the fact that cinema can "resurrect" the dead and make them speak. Today, we see apparitions of Greta Garbo, Cary Grant, Marilyn Monroe. Sure, they're artificial – but we feel close to them. When these actors appear on screen, we don't know what fragrance they were wearing that day, but their gaze testifies to a past that once existed, and in that sense, it serves as an archive. In this aspect, the close-up was revolutionary, because before cinema a sense of proximity to celebrities wasn't possible. Theatre actors and opera stars were generally seen from a distance. Sovereigns showed themselves to the people once a year, and their faces were mostly known through reproductions, thanks to paintings or coins. That's why, for early audiences, the close-up was both enchanting and terrifying.

It's inseparable from the process of stardom that began in the silent era, with Mary Pickford, Charles Chaplin, Greta Garbo...

...and Rudolph Valentino. Some of his admirers went so far as to commit suicide when they heard about his death. If cinema wields such power over people – unlike painting, for example – it's because it creates an intimate connection between the viewer and the image and contains some element of truth, even if it's a "truth" interlaced with lies.

We've taken many theoretical detours, but if you'll permit me, I would like to go back to Whiplash *and, more generally, the reception of your work, starting with that film. It seems to me that it was built around a misunderstanding. Much has been written or said about how your films "praise hard work."*[13]

It's true that your characters strive for success, but this success comes at a price that costs them their personal, emotional or family balance. Your work revolves more around the question of the limits a person is willing to cross in order to realise his dreams – or to live off his art – and the impossible reconciliation with reality. This theme, central in Whiplash, *can also be found in* La La Land, First Man, The Eddy *and* Babylon.

I agree. In Hollywood, there's a whole tradition of films about success. The idealised figure of the self-made man is one of America's foundational myths. But you're right, what interests me more is the price paid to achieve one's dreams. That's what prompted me to make a film about the first man on the Moon, because initially I wasn't that interested in space exploration. I'm much more moved by Neil Armstrong's personal story, all the sacrifices he had to make to pursue his quest. Stepping onto the surface of the Moon elevated humanity to an unprecedented, mythological threshold, but this achievement didn't mark the beginning of a new era. For over fifty years, no one has set foot there again. And if we look at it from the astronauts' perspective, it's a real tragedy. They didn't receive much in return for what they gave. It seems to me that the Apollo 11 mission was an unfulfilled promise. I'm always talking with my editor, Tom Cross, about the epilogues of classic Hollywood movies. Some are disguised as happy endings, when actually they're much less positive than they might seem – like a wolf in sheep's clothing. I like epilogues that work this way. You can be content with what's happening on the surface, but the real outcome is less apparent. Historically, the ending of *First Man* is unquestionably a success, whereas for me, it signifies great sadness. It's a Pyrrhic victory, much like the epilogue of *Whiplash*.

The ending of Whiplash *is indeed very ambiguous because it doesn't provide straightforward answers to the audience. We might think that Fletcher's method eventually bears fruit and that Neiman has truly transcended himself, but you could also conclude that Neiman hasn't escaped the psychological grip of his teacher, or, worse still, that he has made a tacit pact with Fletcher, who displays a sort of Mephistophelian smile in the final shots of the film.*

It's success and failure at the same time, the idea that victory always implies the loss of something. Is it worth it? I like to ask questions, but don't provide definitive answers.

You mentioned your editor, Tom Cross, who has also collaborated with David O. Russell and James Gray. You started working together on the short Whiplash *film, and he has edited all your films since. How does the post-production work? Do you actively participate, or do you let Tom work alone and then show you the finished sequences?*

We share the work. I edited *Guy and Madeline on a Park Bench* on Final Cut Pro, but when we collaborated for the first time, Tom pushed me towards Avid. It took me a few films to understand all its subtleties, but by now I'm well-versed, to the extent that we can work side by side on two different screens.

Do you ask for input from other filmmakers during the editing phase?

Yes. It varies, depending on the films. I showed *Whiplash* and *La La Land* to Jason Reitman, *First Man* to Steven Spielberg, *Babylon* to Mark Romanek and Spike Jonze, who plays the role of a German director in it.

What difficulties did you encounter during the editing of Whiplash*?*

Once again, the main constraint was time. We had only four weeks to finalise the edit so we could submit it to the Sundance Film Festival, and then an additional four weeks for the final edit. We had a lot of shots, and I wanted to find a tempo that matched the music. I knew the editing would be as intense as the shooting, which is why I extensively storyboarded the entire film. I even created animatics from my drawings for each musical sequence. But strictly following the storyboard didn't quite work. When we started editing the final sequence, for example, we realised that being strictly faithful to the animatics eliminated the human dimension, so we rebuilt the sequence by searching for moments in the musical performance that captured the characters' emotions. Tom and I talked a lot about the famous car chase in William Friedkin's *The French Connection*. Everyone remembers the car shots and the tension, but what makes that scene work, fifty years later, is Gene Hackman's face. Without the actor's performance, the sequence falls flat. It seems obvious, but it's something I had to learn during the shooting and editing of *Whiplash*. Regardless, I should emphasise that the editing was mainly a challenge because of the time constraints we faced.

You managed to finish the film for the Sundance Film Festival, where it won the Grand Jury Prize and the Audience Award, then repeated this success at Deauville. And then came the Oscars, where Whiplash *won three awards: Best Supporting Actor for J.K. Simmons, Best Editing and Best Sound Mixing. Commercially, the film grossed $13 million in the US alone, four times its budget. Were you surprised that a film set in the world of jazz was so successful?*

Yes, because when we were making it, our only hope was to be ready to show it at Sundance. When we got there, we thought maybe we could win an award, but it was just a vague intuition. After winning at both Sundance and Deauville, I started to think how great it would be if J.K. Simmons, who had worked hard for so many years without ever winning any awards when he deserved them, was nominated for an Oscar. Just nominated! That was my biggest dream. Everything that happened afterwards was a very pleasant surprise.

1. Justin Hurwitz composed all the non-diegetic music pieces. Tim Simonec was responsible for composing the musical pieces played by Fletcher's ensemble. He also conducted the recordings.
2. See Nathan Réra, *Casualties of War – An Investigation: From Vietnam Atrocity to the Making of Brian De Palma's Masterpiece* (Sticking Place Books, 2024).
3. The issues surrounding this "dispute" over jazz are well summarised by Isabelle Perreault in her article "De l'américanisme en France: le statut paradoxal de la musique jazz (1920-1930)," *Babel*, 28, 2013.
4. Christian Béthune, *Adorno et le jazz, Analyse d'un déni esthétique* (Klincksieck, 2003), 15.
5. Theodor W. Adorno, "On Jazz" (published under the pseudonym Hektor Rottweiler), *Discourse*, vol. 12, no. 1, 1989/1990, 45-69 (translated by Jamie Owen Daniel).
6. This term refers to a purist who cultivates an obsessive interest in jazz, leading them to be out of step with their time musically and develop antisocial tendencies.
7. Richard Brody, "Getting jazz right in the movies," *The New Yorker*, 13 October 2014.
8. Unlike in *Tár* (Todd Field, 2022), which shares many similarities with *Whiplash*. The main character, Lydia Tár (Cate Blanchett), is a renowned conductor who, much like Fletcher, uses her power to favour or harm those in her professional circle, leading to allegations of harassment. Field depicts all the technological means used to undermine her (cell phones, emails, social networks), while subtly avoiding the trap of Manichaeism.
9. *Chronicart*, 13 June 2022.
10. Luc Moullet, "Sur les brisées de Marlowe," *Cahiers du cinéma*, no. 93, 1959.
11. See André Bazin, "Pour un cinéma impur" in *Qu'est-ce que le cinéma?* (Les Éditions du Cerf, 2005), 81-105, and Dork Zabunyan, "Le cinéma, un art impur?" in Jérôme Baron (ed.), *D'autres continents, mouvances du cinéma présent* (Laval, 2018), 89-102.
12. Paraphrase of a line from Charles Baudelaire's "Projet d'un épilogue pour l'édition de 1861" [unfinished] in *Les Fleurs du mal* (Le Livre de poche, 1999), 244.
13. See, for example, Quentin Girard, "Damien Chazelle, le taf des héros," *Libération*, 2 January 2019, and "Damien Chazelle, c'est un peu le Macron du cinéma américain," *La Dispute*, France Culture, 19 October 2018.

DANCING AMONG THE STARS
La La Land

We have already briefly discussed the writing of La La Land *and the difficulties you encountered in finding producers, because of – as you mentioned – the studios' lack of appetite for musicals. I wonder if it wasn't also because of the timeless nature of your screenplay. The story of* La La Land, *focused on the past, is a long way from the kinds of debates that have been rattling around the world of American cinema in recent years, notably issues of "inclusivity." You were also criticised for not casting a black actor in the role of Sebastian and for the lack of gay characters in the film.[1] Any thoughts?*

Let me respond from my position: a white boy who grew up in contemporary America idolising jazz – an art form invented and largely dominated by African-Americans. I'm not an exceptional case. Throughout the twentieth century, there were people who, in a similar way, went through a kind of time warp, culturally and racially, leading them, even though they were white, to become huge fans of black music. Sebastian is a completely irrational comedic character, like the fools and buffoons in Shakespeare's plays. He's the epitome of the obsessive jazz enthusiast, like the character of Chad in Cameron Crowe's *Jerry Maguire*, who proudly presents Jerry with an audio cassette of Miles Davis and John Coltrane's *Live in Stockholm*, claiming – with voice trembling and a burning passion in his eyes – that jazz is "the only American art-form." So much separates him, culturally and temporally, from the music he reveres that it turns him into an almost comical character.

This type of character can't be confined to racial categories, but the typical cliché is a white guy, definitely not a black man. When I sat down to start writing *La La Land*, I sketched several versions of Sebastian and approached every actor in Hollywood who was suitable for the role, both white and black, thinking that the character would eventually adapt to whoever I chose, but in my mind he had to be very different from the musicians in my previous films – people struggling with their own difficulties but who don't hold it against the world, unlike Sebastian, who operates in a sort of temporal no man's land. He's lost in a modern city, perpetually living in the past, and even gets irritated with his sister for sitting in a chair that once belonged to Hoagy Carmichael.[2]

You create his inverse double in the form of Keith, a black musician who offers him a spot in his jazz fusion band. Sebastian eventually accepts, but he sees Keith as a man of compromise. And yet Keith actually has a sensible way of looking at things, and warns Sebastian against his musical narrow-mindedness, which goes against the very principles of jazz.

Yes, Keith is living in the now, and is always pointing out the irony in Sebastian's way of thinking, that he looks down on anyone who doesn't share his vision of music. But what does his hero worship of Thelonious Monk actually achieve? It's one of the key themes of the film. How can someone claim to be revolutionary while being so traditionalist? On the other hand, the film is set in Los Angeles, a city disinterested in its own history. But does that mean we should completely reject the present? We need to strike a balance between preserving the past and moving forward. And this doesn't just apply to music. Through Sebastian, I was trying to confront my own contradictions, my obsession with old films.

At one point, wasn't Miles Teller supposed to play Sebastian?

We did consider that option, yes. In one version of the script, Sebastian was younger, as was Mia, and we offered the role to Emma Watson. I had just finished *Whiplash* and was excited about making another film with Miles because we had such a great time working together. I talked to him about *La La Land* and gradually began discussing the role of Sebastian. Emma Watson then withdrew from the project, and we had to reschedule the shooting dates to find a new actress. Emma Stone came on board, but her schedule didn't line up with Miles'. By that time, I had already met Ryan Gosling because I was also developing *First Man* and considering him for the lead. I remember our first conversation quickly turned to our shared love for musicals, which naturally led us to *La La Land*. For the record, Ryan had already heard about it because long before *Whiplash* I sent him a draft via his agents. We talked about Sebastian's relationship with his sister and his dream of opening a jazz club, and the more we talked, the more it made sense for the character to be in his thirties instead of his twenties. We needed to feel that he had been around the block. Ryan could totally play a jaded Sebastian, worn down by a decade of frustrations, while Miles represented a version of Sebastian just out of adolescence. I eventually decided on Ryan Gosling, which the press misinterpreted.[3] It hasn't stopped me from staying friends with Miles Teller.

A few years earlier, Ryan Gosling had played an adrift musician in Terrence Malick's Song to Song, *filmed in 2012 but released only in 2017, after* La La Land.

I remember talking about it with Ryan, but if I remember rightly, it was after the filming of *La La Land*. At that time, I hadn't yet met Malick.

You met Malick?!

I became friends with him and his wife. We started corresponding during pre-production of *First Man*. I was looking to cast some Texan children in the film, so I travelled to Austin to do auditions and took the opportunity to meet him. We spent a few hours together, during which I asked him every possible question about his work with children on the set of *Tree of Life*. They're extraordinary, aren't they?

Absolutely. Tye Sheridan, who plays one of the boys, is also fantastic in Jeff Nichols' Mud, which he filmed shortly afterwards. Incidentally, a few days ago I rewatched The Tree of Life, *which I disliked when I first saw it, but have since developed a completely new understanding of.*

Oh, really? You aren't the only one who had trouble with *The Tree of Life*. It really divides opinion among the filmmakers I know. What was your issue with it?

I found it artificial, quite pretentious in its attempts to link the intimate and the cosmic. I think I was thrown by the sequence with the dinosaurs, among other things. My own experience of fatherhood probably transformed my perception of the film because today I mainly appreciate Malick's ability to capture the grace, the carefree spirit and the unease of the children. The scene where Brad Pitt plays François Couperin's "Les Barricades Mystérieuses" on the piano, accompanied by his son playing the guitar outside the house on the porch, is moving.

It's such a beautiful sequence! I left the screening astonished, and completely dazzled. The sequences with the children, Brad Pitt and Jessica Chastain's performances, the breathtaking shots of outer space, even the dinosaur sequence – it all makes for an unforgettable piece of cinema. It's only the scenes with Sean Penn that leave me a bit puzzled. The friends I saw it with had a completely different take, but that's exactly what makes the film so interesting: it sparks debate. It's definitely one of my favourite films, to the point where I even rented a 35mm print to show to the *First Man* crew.

Do you like Malick's recent films?

I can't really comment because I haven't seen them. I loved his documentary *Voyage of Time*, and even though *To the Wonder* isn't as good as *The Thin Red Line*, there are some very beautiful things in it. What struck me, particularly around the 2010s, is how Malick's films began to embrace images of contemporary life, of the industrial and commercial world. There are some urban sequences in *The Tree of Life*, but in *To the Wonder* it's the first time we've seen him film gas stations, supermarkets, highways – that kind of thing.

It's something he continues with in Knight of Cups *and* Song to Song *which, together with* To the Wonder, *form a sort of triptych. I remember when* Song to Song *was released, it was labelled as* Zen La La Land, *even though the two films couldn't be more different. You barely see Ryan Gosling making music in Malick's film, unlike in* La La Land, *where he's often at the piano, filmed in long takes, leaving little doubt that it's really him playing.*

Ryan Gosling really impressed me, even though his experience as a musician probably helped.[4] During pre-production, we rehearsed the singing and dancing scenes extensively, but not the piano scenes. Ryan was very secretive about his learning the piano and mostly practiced at home, away from prying eyes, alone or with his piano teacher. I couldn't judge his progress. A few weeks before shooting, I started getting nervous because the only image I had of him at the piano, playing timidly like a beginner, didn't match the image of a professional jazz musician. I was worried that he might not be able to play with the ease and speed required, that he might lack the on-screen flair we needed. And so, to avoid a disaster, we had a backup plan: hand doubles. A few days before shooting started, I put Ryan at the piano with sheet music and said, "Alright, show us what you got." And he played the piece perfectly. I remember filming him with my iPhone, astonished. There was such a gap between what I had seen him do three or four months earlier and the level of proficiency he had reached. He had absorbed the music to the point where he didn't even have to think about where to place his fingers on the keys anymore. Looking back, whatever he did to prepare worked really well, although he got us in trouble because we had hired those hand stand-ins but ended up never using them. We had to pay them not to come on set. [*laughs*] Those are Ryan's hands, even in the close-ups. We never needed the doubles, which saved us a lot of time.

Emma Stone also delivers an accomplished performance, as both an actress and a singer. She had already acted alongside Ryan Gosling, twice, in Crazy, Stupid, Love *and* Gangster Squad *– two largely forgettable films. Did you fear a sense of déjà vu?*

Kind of, yes. When I was working on the script for *La La Land*, neither of those films had been released. I had already conceived the character of Mia with Emma Stone in mind and thought Ryan Gosling would make a good Sebastian, so I sent the script to his agents. While I was re-writing it, *Crazy, Stupid, Love* came out, followed by *Gangster Squad* the year after. I was faced with a dilemma. I had two actors who, separately, were perfect for the roles, but they had just acted together twice, and both in films set in Los Angeles. When Emma Stone came on board after Emma Watson stepped away, I suggested reuniting her with Ryan one more time, and she liked the idea. Later I talked to Ryan about it, and he was excited, so I realised I had the opportunity to recreate a sort of old-school duo, something you hardly ever see in Hollywood anymore. I had in mind all these magical pairings from the classic era: Ginger Rogers and Fred Astaire, of course, but also Judy Garland and Mickey Rooney, Lauren Bacall and Humphrey Bogart, Myrna Loy and William Powell. Since *La La Land* was about old movies, it was only logical to try and recreate a kind of timeless duo, very different from the idea we have of actors since the creation of the Actors Studio.

Emma and Ryan loved the idea, especially as they were convinced that their collaboration in the previous two films hadn't allowed them to explore their full potential. They were eager to explore more of what they could do together, and *La La Land* was the perfect playground for that.

The scenes where Emma Stone goes from one audition to another, facing humiliation after humiliation, are inspired by her own experiences, as well as Ryan Gosling's. Talk about your approach to casting. Do you usually attend auditions? Have you ever offered a role without an audition?

That has happened, yes. It depends on the situation. I've offered roles to actors I knew well without asking them to audition. On the other hand, even if I'm familiar with an actor's work, sometimes it's important to audition them. It doesn't have to be a formal one – a simple conversation can be enough. I've also auditioned unknowns, and to be honest I'm not too fond of the process. I find it tough, and a bit cruel. I'd like to think that as a filmmaker I should make the experience as pleasant as possible for the actors – but it doesn't ever really happen. They're putting themselves out there emotionally in front of strangers who, after the audition, usually just say, "Thanks, we'll let you know." And in 99 percent of cases, it's a no. So it can be tough, because it's both very intimate and incredibly intimidating, very real yet very artificial at the same time. It's the least glamorous part of Hollywood, and I thought it made sense to show that contrast in a romantic musical.

There are two professional musicians in La La Land*. One is D.A. Wallach, your former colleague from Chester French, who plays a parody of himself in the party sequence where Mia and Sebastian meet, and John Legend, who plays Keith. How did you come to cast them?*

Justin Hurwitz suggested that I give a small role to D.A. Wallach, and I immediately loved the idea. As for John Legend, I remember suggesting that we meet, but it wasn't a formal audition, just a chat that was useful in helping me develop the scene where Keith talks with Sebastian about their perspectives on music. John Legend is quite fascinating. He's a virtuoso trained in jazz and classical music, yet chose to express himself in a popular, contemporary and accessible style, all while tipping his hat to the traditions of African-American singers and pianists. The perspective he brought to Keith was spot on, to the extent that the words spoken by his character in the film are essentially his own. Whenever possible, I like working with people who, in real life, do the same job as the people they're playing on screen, not because I'm aiming for some pseudo "authenticity," but because I'm convinced that their way of dressing, speaking and behaving can inform or enrich the role. And it makes the film more layered because it feels like each character has their own world that exists beyond the screen, even if we only catch a glimpse of that world – a small portion that the filmmaker chooses to bring into the frame.

It was playful of you to have Keith play the guitar instead of the piano, which is John Legend's instrument of choice. On one hand, as in your other films, you have transformed real musicians into actors, and on the other you have actors playing musicians, singers and dancers. Ryan Gosling and Emma Stone do tap dance, but they aren't quite at the level of Fred Astaire and Ginger Rogers. With your choreographer Mandy Moore, it seems that you're intentionally highlighting their awkwardness, just as with the songs they sing.

Mandy Moore, who's a very relaxed choreographer, is used to working with actors who aren't dancers, as she did on David O. Russell's films *American Hustle* and *Joy*, which – although they're not musicals – include dance sequences. Our approach on *La La Land* was similar to that of *Guy and Madeline on a Park Bench*, except that we drew from slightly different sources. For *Guy and Madeline*, we looked at black-and-white musicals in the 4:3 ratio, back when the genre was still new, but with *La La Land* we looked at musicals from the late 1950s and early 1960s, in Technicolor, produced by MGM. Of course, we sprinkled in references to those Ginger and Fred films from the 1930s, but aesthetically we wanted that lush Technicolor palette of classic musicals while maintaining a certain naturalism that came from the actors and settings. The song and dance sequences also fit into this quest for naturalism. We didn't jazz them up or edit any voices. We wanted it a bit raw, not perfect. I was really into this clash between the classic musical style and these characters who aren't naturally part of that world. Mia and Sebastian aren't Ginger and Fred, even if they might want to be like them, and the city they're in isn't some postcard Paris from *Love Me Tonight*. It's a car-clogged, anti-romantic megalopolis where their love story ends badly.

For all these reasons, it was important to have a choreographer who didn't just mechanically teach the actors dance steps. Mandy first studied how Ryan and Emma naturally moved, so that the choreography could emerge organically from their bodies. It was a very fluid process. Ryan and Emma made suggestions, sometimes they would improvise, and Mandy would observe and guide them. She taught them dance steps that we didn't plan to use in the film, just to see how their bodies reacted. Occasionally, Ryan or Emma would perform a funny or surprising movement or gesture that Mandy would incorporate into the dance numbers. Apart from the final ballet, each number had a real setting, which is the opposite of traditional musicals, where real locations were reconstructed in the studio. There were some problems doing it that way, for example the scene where Ryan and Emma sing "A Lovely Night," which was shot at the top of a hill overlooking Los Angeles. The road was on a slope, making it more difficult for them to dance, and we didn't use any artificial lighting, so we had twenty minutes to film with the sunset in the background. All these constraints made perfection an impossibility, but offered something even more important: the tension that arose from the encounter between reality and artifice.

Along with Ryan Gosling, Emma Stone and Mandy Moore, you paid a visit to Patricia Ward Kelly, Gene Kelly's last wife, before the start of filming. Why was that important?

It was essential for us to capture the spirit of Gene Kelly in *La La Land*, even if we didn't want to imitate him, and juxtapose that spirit with the everyday, which is an idea you see in some classic Hollywood films like *On the Town*, where Gene Kelly and his partners dance with trash can lids, or in Charles Walters' *Summer Stock*, where he dances on a sheet of newspaper on a creaky floor. I love this in musicals: paying attention to everyday things that aren't extravagant or romantic, just down-to-earth.

In La La Land, *there are two forces that attract and repel each other: poetry on the one hand, banality on the other. During pre-production, you actually sketched a linear graph where a curve, symbolising the characters' trajectory, oscillates between "imagination" and "reality."[5] The moments corresponding to the imaginary line are the opening, the planetarium sequence and the final ballet, while the traffic jam, the failed audition and the dinner that turns into an argument are moments where the characters are firmly within reality.*

I sketched that graph to guide my discussions with the costume designer, choreographer, cinematographer and set designers. It later proved useful during filming because we didn't shoot in chronological order and it was essential to know where we were in the overall scheme. It was a bit schizophrenic. One day we felt like we were shooting a musical because everything was pure artifice, then the next day we were filming in a small room – a failed audition or a quarrel. I didn't want there to be a clear separation between the dance sequences, the songs and the rest of the story, unlike what you might see in *Pennies from Heaven* or *Dancer in the Dark*. As with Demy's films, the line between imagination and reality had to be blurred, which is why the non-musical long shots were filmed like dance scenes, and conventional dialogue like sung passages.[6] This made the moments of rupture even more striking. Sebastian and Mia's failed dinner, culminating in their argument, is the first moment in the film where the camera isn't in motion. The scene is filmed very statically, in a shot/reverse shot, and the music stops, giving way to a heavy silence.

We'll come back to that sequence. I note that the narrative construction of La La Land *is symmetrically opposite to that of* Guy and Madeline on a Park Bench. *In your first film, the two characters part ways at the beginning and eventually reunite at the end, suggesting that their love story might be rekindled, while in* La La Land, *they meet, share a part of their life journey together, but eventually separate, and the final reunion doesn't change that. These are two films I would describe as "false twins." Do you look at* Guy and Madeline *as a kind of dry run for* La La Land?

Yes, because they share the same starting point: *The Umbrellas of Cherbourg*. Both films are pushing the idea that unfinished romances are the most romantic love stories. Feelings of longing, loss and absence make for poetry that doesn't exist in happily-ever-after love stories. We're transported into the realm of imagination: "What if…? What would have happened if…?" There are some works I consider foundational in this respect: Maupassant's short stories, Renoir's *A Day in the Country*, Rohmer's *My Night at Maud's*. They belong to this very French tradition of romantic melancholy, which speaks of what didn't happen but that we wished would have unfolded. This relationship between past regrets and present disappointment, which I find very powerful, was the central theme of *Guy and Madeline* and *La La Land*, as well as in all the unfinished musicals I wrote in between.

La La Land *was shot in forty days, twice the time it took to make* Whiplash. *Did this mean any changes in your approach, like the number of takes you allowed yourself?*

The challenge in *Whiplash* was to get as many shots as possible in the shortest amount of time. The philosophy of

La La Land was very different since we primarily used long takes. There were sometimes cutaway shots, but most of the time we tried to cut in camera. The way of achieving this was simple: rehearsal, rehearsal, rehearsal. I knew I wouldn't be able to hide my mistakes with editing. When we arrived on set, we rehearsed and timed the dialogue to synchronise it with the camera movement. Once everything was set, we started shooting, with a similar objective to *Whiplash*: to nail two excellent takes. The long takes were so complex that we ended up needing a lot more than two to get them right. For *Whiplash*, we rarely shot more than six or seven takes, but for *La La Land* we did twenty, thirty, even forty takes – sometimes forty-five. But since the number of shots was reduced, we had the time. It's mathematical: fewer shots, more takes.

We haven't yet talked about the opening of La La Land, *which is a landmark moment in the history of musicals. You spent two days filming it on the access ramp of a highway interchange under unfavourable weather conditions: scorching sun and strong wind. It's a tour de force that gives the illusion of a continuous shot.*

There are two hidden cuts which are done with whip-pans. We also used morphing for the highway shot that follows the one where the title appears. They were shot on different days. The visual effects team did a good job hiding it.

In cinema, the motif of a traffic jam rarely generates positive, communicative energy. It often serves as a critique of consumer society, as seen in films like Jacques Tati's Trafic *and Luigi Comencini's* Traffic Jam, *or leads us to a nightmarish world, as in Jean-Luc Godard's* Weekend *and David Cronenberg's* Crash *and* Cosmopolis.

The most annoying thing about Los Angeles is the traffic. The idea was to take elements of the city that seemed the least appealing and turn them into joyful emotions. But joy – the driving force behind musicals – lacks depth if it doesn't contain some element of sadness. This is what distinguishes forgettable musicals from those that reach the heights of cinematic art. Take, for example, the famous sequence from *Top Hat* where Jerry Travers [Fred Astaire] finds himself in a ballroom with Dale Tremont [Ginger Rogers]. She's convinced that he's in love with another woman, and he thinks he's about to lose her. She's disoriented, annoyed and disappointed, but as they start to dance and Jerry sings "Cheek to Cheek," her sadness is replaced by a feeling of fulfilment, to the point that by the end of their number, they seem completely in love. *Top Hat* isn't *Singin' in the Rain* – it's a small operetta of sorts. But for me, this scene is one of the pinnacles of the musical genre, and I would rush to show it to anyone unfamiliar with or dismissive of the genre. Astaire and Rogers work true magic by turning this very ordinary, if not downright cheesy moment, into a moment of pure poetry. There's a similar idea at the beginning of *La La Land*. The drivers stuck in their cars in the middle of the traffic jam suddenly forget their troubles and start singing a ridiculous song together. There's nothing more absurd. The real challenge was to turn this silly situation into a sublime moment, elevated by music, choreography and direction.

Coming back to *Top Hat*, I'm fascinated by how Ginger Rogers is once again captivated by a sense of longing when Fred Astaire finishes singing "Cheek to Cheek." There's this idea that at a certain point, the daydream has to end and we have to confront reality. Look at *Meet Me in St. Louis* or *On the Town*. I made it a guiding principle. Immediately after the opening of *La La Land*, the drivers return to their cars and go back to their lives, reconnecting with the negativity of the initial images: killing time in a traffic jam. The lyrics of the song tell the same story: living with dashed hopes ("and even when the answer's no"), money problems ("when my money's running low"), chasing after illusions ("chasing all the lights that shine"). Even the chorus of the song – "It's another day of sun" – has a double meaning: tomorrow is another day, which seems positive, but in an endless city that resembles an unforgiving purgatory. Justin Hurwitz's music reflects this ambivalence well. There isn't a single piece in the film that doesn't play with the relationship between major and minor keys. I remember telling Justin every time he played me melodies on the piano, "Wow – this is so sad!" "Another Day of Sun," for instance, seems very cheerful in its orchestral version, with brass and percussion, but when played as a solo piano piece, at a slower pace, it's a sad song. For this, we owe much to Michel Legrand and Jacques Demy. The melodies of *La La Land* are very much French-inspired.

The audio commentary you recorded with Justin Hurwitz for the DVD release of La La Land *is enlightening, both about your working relationship and how the film was made. Justin explains how he played pieces directly on set during filming. What were the advantages of him doing that?*

We stumbled upon it by chance. We wanted a real connection to develop between the singer and the accompanist in the more intimate sequences, like the jazz club. We used this approach for the scene where Emma and Ryan sing "City of Stars" and for the one where Emma performs "Audition (The Fools Who Dream)," so that the interplay between instrument and voice wouldn't seem artificial – especially in the latter case, because the song is rubato. Justin would be behind the camera, at the keyboard, or sometimes even in another room, wearing an earpiece, as Emma was, which allowed them to hear each other. We used this technique on *Guy and Madeline on a Park Bench*.

You mentioned earlier that you had drafted provisional lyrics for the songs before lyricists Benj Pasek and Justin Paul came in to rewrite them. How did your collaboration unfold?

I don't remember if I showed them the provisional lyrics, but I don't think I did because I really wanted them to start from scratch. In many cases, I had written provisional lyrics for pieces that we ultimately discarded, and some pieces had no lyrics at all. Pasek and Paul listened to the melodies and read the screenplay, and I shared certain ideas I wanted to see them explore in the songs, in terms of narrative and themes. It was tricky because Justin's melodies, which are really ornate, are full of small loops that sometimes make it challenging to fit lyrics to. There were times when Pasek and Paul found words I really liked, but they required Justin to make rhythmic changes in the melody, or we had to add a section to the song to accommodate another idea in the lyrics. There was a lot of back and forth between the four of us. It was a genuine collaboration. In the end, the DNA of the melodies that Justin composed remained intact.

Justin said that he composed a monumental 1,900 piano demos for the film! You only used a tiny fraction. I believe the catchy, whistled melody accompanying the De'Longhi advertisement with Brad Pitt that you directed was originally intended for La La Land.

It was an old song written for one of the earlier versions of the *La La Land* script, a ballad for Emma's character, but Justin and I felt we needed something stronger, so we ended up shelving it in favour of "City of Stars." Since *Guy and Madeline*, we've maintained a repertoire of all the melodies we haven't used, regularly readapting pieces for films or commercials. That's actually what we did for *Babylon*.

It creates a sonic circulation between your films, as if they have emerged from the same stream.

I like that idea. I hadn't thought about it…

J.K. Simmons' cameo in La La Land *also contributes to this sense that your films aren't isolated, but somehow all connected.*

It's more unconscious than conscious, but I'm intrigued by the way films interrelate to form a single work. I like the idea of revisiting certain characters, like Balzac does in *La Comédie humaine*.

But there's something else that needs exploring, which Babylon *might also be tied into: the character briefly played by J.K. Simmons in* La La Land, *the restaurant owner who hates jazz, is a caricature of Fletcher in* Whiplash. *There's a certain self-mockery to it.*

Exactly! I embrace self-mockery.

Let's talk a bit about the pictorial quality of La La Land, *which is as much about the trompe-l'oeil settings and the murals the characters pass by as it is the indirect nods to paintings. The shots of cinema facades or cafes are reminiscent of Edward Hopper, and the planetarium sequence, often compared to other musicals,[7] brings to mind the poetry of Marc Chagall's flying lovers.*

Hopper and Chagall are certainly two important references for me. I've also studied Californian painting very closely, especially Ed Ruscha's gas stations, which directly links to the epilogue of *The Umbrellas of Cherbourg*. Of course, they're nothing alike in terms of scale compared to the small Esso gas station where Catherine Deneuve meets Nino Castelnuovo. The Los Angeles gas stations are huge and lit up at night – beautiful and ugly at the same time. I like this duality of Ruscha's works. Los Angeles isn't really a city, it's an imaginary expanse stretching to the horizon, between the desert and the beach, with no seasons and palm trees in winter. This unreal dimension is especially well rendered in Ruscha's paintings, and David Hockney's too.[8]

Have you ever discussed this with Linus Sandgren?

Yes. Linus is a big photography enthusiast, especially Gregory Crewdson and William Eggleston.

You're loyal to most of your technicians, but I noticed you like to change your production designer depending on the subject of your films. For La La Land, *you worked with David and Sandy Wasco, who for two decades were close collaborators of Quentin Tarantino. Why did you choose them?*

I love their work in Tarantino's films, especially in *Pulp Fiction*, where the backdrop is a sort of cinematic, but also authentic, Los Angeles. You feel it especially in the sequence where Bruce Willis is filmed in a continuous shot, walking from his car to his apartment. It's one of the things sorely lacking in most films that have tried to imitate the style of *Pulp Fiction*, which is why I really wanted to work with the Wascos. I wanted the visuals and sets to move between a fairy-tale and a documentary.

The same goes for the costumes, which are sometimes very ordinary, sometimes very artificial and colourful. It's almost as if you and costume designer Mary Zophres were painting on film.

As with the sets, it was important to strike a balance. To expand on what you said about colours, I've always found that the most beautiful colour films were the early ones, like *The Adventures of Robin Hood*, *Gone with the Wind* and *Meet Me in St. Louis*, where you feel the touch of Natalie Kalmus, who was a colour specialist for the Technicolor process. I'm thinking also of Powell and Pressburger's films, like *Black Narcissus* and *The Red Shoes*, photographed by Jack Cardiff. The magic of the early colour films has faded over the decades, mainly for chemical reasons. The two-colour or three-colour Technicolor gave a surreal quality to colours, which is fascinating for us, as we're used to more natural colours. Over time, colour was taken for granted, verisimilitude became the norm, and there came a moment when we didn't even think about colours, similar to what happened with sound after the advent of sound in films. There were a few exceptions, like Jacques Demy's films.

I wanted to change this relative disinterest in colour, to the point of making it a fundamental element of *La La Land*'s aesthetics. During pre-production, Mary Zophres, Linus Sandgren, the Wascos and I spent an entire week talking only about colour. Based on the script, scene by scene, we defined the colours, their function, their symbolism in the film. We decided, for example, that in the planetarium sequence, Mia would wear a green dress. Since it was the culmination of her love story with Sebastian, we concluded that the colour green should play a significant role not only for the character but also for the development of the love story. During our brainstorming sessions, we discussed a lot of ideas, some of which we kept and some we junked. While filming we continued talking about colour. When it came to the grading stage, I had fascinating conversations with my colourist, Natasha Léonnet. We wanted to give the impression of literally sensing the film's colours, as if they had the smell and texture of fresh paint. It was all about finding the right balance because in some places they seemed oversaturated. They had to feel like they organically emanated from the things we were filming, so we experimented and came to understand, for example, that to make the colours come from the clothing and objects rather than from the lighting or camera, we needed to use white light.

You mentioned Mia's green dress. I'm reminded of another green: the one that appears twice in Sebastian's apartment, first when he's singing "City of Stars" with Mia, and then during the dinner scene that turns into a big fight, leading to their break-up. When I first saw La La Land *in the cinema, the greenish light in these two scenes immediately caught my eye because it reminded me of* Vertigo, *where a neon light illuminates Judy Barton's room. I rewatched Hitchcock's film and my initial hunch was right: the same curtains, the same eerie light. In* Vertigo, *the colour green is symbolically linked to the return of the dead Madeleine, "reincarnated" as Judy, and simultaneously to the impossibility of the all-consuming blind love that Scottie has for Madeleine in the first part of the film. From the moment he tries to make Judy look like the dead woman, his love turns into morbid obsession and dooms their passionate relationship. Symbolically, green is an ambivalent colour: it signifies life, luck and dreams, and at the same time misfortune, poison and the devil.[9] When Mia and Sebastian sing "City of Stars" bathed in* Vertigo's *green light, it's as if their romance is already haunted by misfortune. Their love literally falls apart before our eyes in that dinner scene, where the green contaminates everything, from the scenery decor to their faces. It's under the negative influence of this green that the music stops, the cake burns in the oven, and Mia gets up and slams the door.*

I'd love to say that I thought about the symbolic value of colours in this scene, but truthfully, I simply reacted instinctively to my visual intuitions. We never talked about *Vertigo* during pre-production on *La La Land*, and that reference to the film almost didn't happen. It was only the day before shooting the apartment scene that I felt something was missing, and I had an epiphany when I watched *Vertigo* again. My favourite shot in the film comes just before Judy transforms into Madeleine, when she's sitting by the window, with the lights outside, and you can only see her silhouette in the dim light, wearing a purple dress. What appears symbolic in hindsight is often initially very unconscious because we respond to images based on our tastes and preferences. In this case, what fascinated me in that shot was the combination of green and purple. One thing I discovered while working on *La La Land* is that it's not so much about isolating one colour as it is about getting colours to interact with each other because they mutually influence each other. This is self-evident for anyone versed in the science of colours. Our perception of blue changes depending on whether it's paired with yellow or red, and purple makes green look even more beautiful. I called Linus at two in the morning the night before the shoot and asked him to set up a green curtain and light it in a way that its colour would bleed into the set, and asked Mary Zophres to find me a purple dress.

The scene where Mia and her husband leave for the evening and say goodbye to the babysitter taking care of their daughter reminds me of a similar scene at the opening of Stanley Kubrick's Eyes Wide Shut. *Later on, by chance, the couple ends up in Sebastian's jazz club, just as in* Eyes Wide Shut *Bill Hartford ends up at the Sonata Café during his nocturnal wanderings, where one of his former university friends, pianist Nick Nightingale, is performing.*

I wasn't specifically thinking of *Eyes Wide Shut*, but that film certainly inspired me in terms of colours, as well as the idea of a city caught between reality and imagination. I remember when *Eyes Wide Shut* came out, some critics said, "It has nothing to do with New York, the film was shot in London." And yet that's precisely why the film is so beautiful and fascinating. It resembles New York, but it's a dreamlike rendition, and is strangely unsettling.

Do you agree that La La Land, *in part, embodies what one might call "postmodern," with all the reg flags associated with that term?*[10] *It's a work rich in references, characterised by a certain intermingling – a notion Perry Anderson defines as a celebration of "the crossover, the hybrid, the pot-pourri." In essence, every image conceals another, but this awareness isn't just synonymous with aesthetic pleasure. It evokes a sort of melancholic vertigo regarding past artistic forms. Saying this brings to mind Umberto Eco's masterful definition of postmodernity: "I think of the postmodern attitude as that of a man who loves a very cultivated woman and knows that he cannot say to her 'I love you madly,' because he knows that she knows (and that she knows he knows) that these words have already been written by Barbara Cartland. Still, there is a solution. He can say, 'As Barbara Cartland would put it, I love you madly.' At this point, having avoided false innocence, having said clearly it is no longer possible to speak innocently, he will nevertheless have said what he wanted to say to the woman: that he loves her in an age of lost innocence."*[11] *This quote seems to illustrate the tension present in* La La Land *between the 1940s and '50s musicals and your reinterpretation of the genre. To put it simply, your film could never have ended in the same way as Vincente Minnelli's* The Band Wagon, *where the thwarted romance between Tony and Gabrielle is resolved and everyone euphorically sings, "The world is a stage, the stage is a world of entertainment." In* La La Land, *Mia and Sebastian, who will never get back together, exchange one last look and part ways forever, "like two ships passing in the night" – as you put it in the DVD commentary for the film.*

I love that line from Umberto Eco. I've never heard it before. How about this one, about *Casablanca*, where Eco writes: "Two clichés make us laugh. A hundred clichés move us."[12] That's such a great idea. Something deep, honest and beautiful emerges when clichés interact with each other. That's one of the reasons I love musicals so much. Despite being the most artificial of genres, packed with clichés, musicals often stir up deeper emotions than many so-called "realistic" films. Realism can become quite limiting, whereas musicals break free because they aren't bound by life's everyday rules. It all comes back to this ultimate contradiction, which interests me more than anything: creating reality through artifice and finding beauty in clichés. How do you believe in two characters telling each other "I love you" even though you've seen it in a thousand other films? It's the impossibility of being completely innovative that creates the conditions for beauty.

You mentioned being anxious before La La Land *was screened at the Venice Film Festival, where it was warmly received and where Emma Stone won the Volpi Cup for Best Actress. Then came the Golden Globes and the Oscars. How do you handle the pressure of public attention and awards?*

I think the right attitude is not to worry about it, and once the awards are over, regardless of their outcome, just move on and forget about them. But it's a bit of an inner struggle because the desire for recognition is part of human nature.

The Oscars ceremony, where La La Land *won six awards, featured the incredible mix-up when it came to the Best Picture award, which was initially given to your film before being correctly handed to Barry Jenkins'* Moonlight. *The entire* La La Land *crew had time to take the stage and your producers delivered their thank-you speeches before the mistake made by Warren Beatty and Faye Dunaway – who presented the award – was revealed.*

That was very strange. I had an odd night. I was sick and feverish that day, in a kind of daze. A journalist asked me, "Wasn't it great to hear your name when you got the Oscar?" What a question! Obviously I was grateful to the Academy, but at that moment there was no pleasure, no particular happiness. It was actually really stressful because when you're standing there, you know you have to say something but you're just hoping you don't screw up. Up on the stage you can't hear anything and can barely see the audience. The real emotions come later – once the ceremony is over. At the time it's like being in a dream. I don't even remember what I said in my speech.

You started by thanking the other nominated filmmakers, among them Denis Villeneuve for Arrival, *which is one of the most beautiful science-fiction films in recent years.*

I really admire Denis' work. He's also a very generous guy – which doesn't take away from his talent. Amidst all the nonsense of these ceremonies, there's something really great: the chance to meet other filmmakers and exchanges ideas with them, build friendships. Apart from that, I find the award system pretty weird. The best way to navigate it is to stay on target with the work and not let yourself be overcome by success, which can certainly be intoxicating.

Among the encounters made possible by La La Land *was one with Michel Legrand, during a screening of your film in Paris in December 2016, which you described as the "most intense moment" of your filmmaking journey. He later honoured you by entrusting you with writing the preface for his autobiography, which is surely a huge accolade.*

Michel Legrand was very nice, as was his wife, Macha Méril, who I have stayed in touch with. I also got to know Agnès Varda and her children, Mathieu and Rosalie. Having been able to meet some of my heroes is one of the most extraordinary things I've taken away from my *La La Land* experience.

1. See Noah Gittell, "The *La La Land* backlash," *The Guardian*, 6 February 2017, and Steve Chambers, "*La La Land* Is Clueless About What's Actually Happening in Jazz," *Vulture*, 13 January 2017.
2. Composer, jazz pianist and singer Hoagy Carmichael (1899-1981) wrote some classics of the American songbook, including "Georgia on My Mind," which is widely known thanks to Ray Charles' 1960 version. He also acted in *To Have and Have Not* (Howard Hawks, 1944) and *The Best Years of Our Lives* (William Wyler, 1946).
3. This misunderstanding appears to have been fuelled by Miles Teller himself. See Anna Peele, "Miles Teller Is Young, Talented, and Doesn't Give a Rat's Ass What You Think," *Esquire*, 5 August 2015.
4. In the late 2000s, Ryan Gosling founded a rock band called Dead Man's Bones with Zach Shields. He served as both the lead singer and guitarist for the group. The duo released their debut album in 2009.
5. See Damien Chazelle, "De la vie réelle à la vie rêvée" in N.T. Binh (ed.), *Comédies musicales, la joie de vivre du cinéma* (Éditions de la Martinière, 2018), 19.
6. Chazelle develops this idea in Franck Garbatz, "Un sentiment d'ivresse comme lorsqu'on est amoureux ou que ses rêves ne se réalisent pas," *Positif*, January 2017.
7. See the numerous connections made by Simone Tarditi in *La La Land de Damien Chazelle* (Gremese, 2020), 80-81.
8. Ruscha has delved deeply into the relationships between landscape, architecture and culture, including the Hollywood sign, which he has reproduced in several of his works that lie at the intersection of Pop Art and conceptual art. As for Hockney's famous swimming pools, they have become emblematic of a hedonistic California characterised by a certain emptiness, as suggested by the pool party scene where neither Mia nor Sebastian feel comfortable.
9. See Michel Pastoureau, *Vert: histoire d'une couleur* (Éditions Points, 2019).
10. The complexity and various meanings of this concept are discussed in Perry Anderson, *The Origins of Postmodernity* (Verso, 1998).
11. Umberto Eco, *Postscript to The Name of the Rose* (Harcourt Brace Jovanovich, 1984), 67.
12. Umberto Eco, "*Casablanca*, or the Clichés Are Having a Ball" in Marshall Blonsky (ed.), *On Signs* (Johns Hopkins, 1985), 38.

A TRIP TO THE END OF THE MOON
First Man

It's almost mid-October, and you can see the end of the Babylon tunnel.

I can't wait to finish the edit. We only have one more week left. But since I've been saying this for months, I remain cautious…

The trailer has been released, and I have to admit it caught me off-guard. I thought Babylon *would be a melodramatic epic, not quite so offbeat. Despite the internal coherence of your work, you always seem to end up in the most unexpected places.* Whiplash *is the antithesis of* Guy and Madeline on a Park Bench, *just as* La La Land, *in some way, is the antithesis of* Whiplash. *Those three films got you pigeonholed as a director known for always designing his films around music.* First Man *was a radical shift in terms of subject and genre – and now again with* Babylon. *Is this reinvention, this constant reshuffling of the cards and blurring of the lines, conscious and intentional?*

Most of the time it's unconscious. Because each film is an intense experience that takes up all my time, I'm always feeling the need to move in new directions, to change things around and do the opposite of what I've been doing. I'm aware of the evolution of my work, but I'm more instinctive and not so calculating. I tend to go with however I feel in the moment.

Do you ever rewatch your films, or are you one of those filmmakers for whom it's torture because you see only the imperfections?

I'm sometimes obliged to rewatch my films, to check the versions that are being distributed. It's not necessarily something I enjoy doing because I always notice things that bother me, and I certainly understand the kind of anxiety you're talking about. But that doesn't mean I would ever consider changing my films once they're done. I'm not a fan of the "director's cut," except in cases where the director lost control of the editing. I would have loved to see the final cut of Erich von Stroheim's *Greed* or Orson Welles' *The Magnificent Ambersons*. But for a filmmaker to decide, ten or twenty years later, to re-edit their film seems problematic to me.

That's what Coppola did for the thirtieth anniversary of The Godfather, Part III, *when he rolled out a new edit, which was twenty minutes shorter than the original, supposedly more in line with his initial intentions and those of the novel's author, Mario Puzo. He changed crucial parts of the film and even removed the final image. Those who think – and I'm one of them – that the original 1990 version is an underestimated masterpiece weren't pleased.*

I completely agree. It's a way of rewriting history, and it bothers me.

Let's talk about First Man, *which is a pivotal entry in your filmography. It's your first film that's not centred around music and your first historical drama, based on James Hansen's authorised biography of Neil Armstrong.[1] Warner acquired the rights in the early 2000s and Clint Eastwood was set to direct, before the project moved to Universal and was developed by producers Wyck Godfrey and Isaac Klausner, who had previously collaborated on* The Twilight Saga. *When did you first hear about it?*

Back when I was a screenwriter, in the early 2010s. I knew Wyck and Isaac. During one of our meetings, they mentioned a film project about Neil Armstrong, but it wasn't until the success of *Whiplash* at Sundance that they asked me to direct it.

Why do you think it took so long for Neil Armstrong's epic to attract the attention of major Hollywood studios? Films like Philip Kaufman's The Right Stuff *and Ron Howard's* Apollo 13 *depicted the space race long ago.*

It's difficult to tell a story that everyone knows, especially with so few characters. It's nothing like the sinking of the Titanic, for example, which had more than two thousand passengers. Many died, but some survived – which offers infinite possibilities to imagine unique storylines and create moments of suspense. As for the Apollo 11 mission, only two astronauts landed on the Moon. Their journey was filmed, photographed and widely publicised, instantly becoming part of popular culture, and – importantly – the mission was a success, so there's not much of a story to tell. *The Right Stuff* is focused on Chuck Yeager's early space flights, which were by no means as well known to the public as Armstrong was, and *Apollo 13* deals with the incident that led to the failure of the mission, is a suspense film. For all these reasons, when the producers proposed a film about Neil Armstrong, I wasn't interested. A documentary seemed a much better way of capturing the poetry and symbolism of the event, and that had already been done by Al Reinert in *For All Mankind* – a masterpiece in its own right.

What made you change your mind?

I ended up thinking: the only way to tell the story of the first step on the Moon, one of the greatest achievements in human history, is to make a film about failure. There was the loss of Armstrong's daughter, then this succession of failures and violent deaths that paved the way to the Moon. Elliot See and Charles Bassett perished during preparation for the Gemini 9 mission. Ed White, Gus Grissom and Roger Chaffee died in the spacecraft fire during a test for the Apollo 1 mission. In a way, these events marked the end of innocence for space exploration, not to mention that towards the end of the 1960s, amid the context of the Vietnam War, American public opinion was largely against the project. The idea that the Moon landing could have been a tragedy, not just for Neil Armstrong but also for all those around him, particularly interested me. I don't mean to say that space exploration wasn't worth it, but I do see a certain sadness in this quest that I haven't seen in any other film. I'm fascinated by this kind of paradox – it's a bit like making an exuberant musical about an unhappy love story. The arrival of the first man on the Moon was met with indescribable jubilation, but I wanted the audience to feel a deep sadness at the end of *First Man*. If audiences don't feel this affliction, it means I didn't really achieve my goal.

Not only do I feel it in the epilogue, but I experience it throughout the film.

Well, that's good. It probably explains why the film didn't do well commercially.

First Man *is, to date, the only one of your feature films which you didn't write. Why is that?*

The original plan was for me to write the adaptation, but there was a lot of research that needed to be done, and not being a historian or a journalist, I pretty quickly figured out that having the help of a screenwriter with experience of working with historical material would be useful. We had to navigate the wealth of sources available to us and carve a path to avoid getting completely lost. I can't remember if the idea of contacting Josh Singer came from me or the producers. We hit it off from our very first meeting. Research actually began in parallel with the development of *La La Land*, and we went to Houston to scout locations. Josh did a great job researching the history.

How did the writing go?

We worked together on the treatment, and after agreeing on the structure of the screenplay, Josh began writing. The timing was good because due to the filming of *La La Land*, I wasn't around for several months. Josh sent me the finished screenplay during post-production, and we did revisions together while I was editing. Josh would send me successive drafts, I would read them and give him my suggestions, then he would make the corrections and send me the modified version. Sometimes we were in the same room, which allowed Josh to make changes and present them to me on the spot. I also visited him on the set of Steven Spielberg's *The Post*, where we took advantage of moments between takes to refine the script and make small adjustments to the dialogue. This way of working suited me because even though I didn't write the script, I felt very involved and wouldn't have been able to direct the film otherwise.

Steven Spielberg was an executive producer on First Man. *What was his involvement during the film's production?*

Spielberg – who had already collaborated with Josh Singer on several other projects – read the screenplay and suggested that the film be a Universal/Dreamworks co-production. He's very friendly and approachable. I visited him during pre-production to get advice on how to film the rocket launch. In most recent films it's the kind of thing that's done with CGI, but I've never really liked the look of it. Even though I couldn't completely forgo digital effects, I wanted to shoot in a real environment, with models, and since I had never done that before, Spielberg's expertise was invaluable. After filming he came to the edit once or twice, then I showed him the finished film. I needed this kind of support because I was worried about the studio's reaction.

What were your concerns?

I didn't know if the studio would be willing to accept that the tone of the film wasn't triumphant, that Neil Armstrong's story was being told as a tragedy. And some of our artistic choices were contested. The studio heads, who had seen the rushes, weren't overly enthusiastic about a good portion of the film being shot in 16mm. But that was nothing compared to their reaction when they heard the music for the first time – which they hated. It was a struggle to get our way. I won the war, but it wasn't easy, especially for Justin.

I'm surprised to hear that, because the music in First Man, which earned Justin Hurwitz a third Golden Globe, is so moving. He uses unconventional instruments, like the theremin, which Neil Armstrong particularly liked. Armstrong even took Harry Revel's album Music Out of the Moon, *recorded with theremin player Samuel J. Hoffman, on the journey to the Moon. In* First Man *we see Armstrong putting the record on at home and dancing with his wife to the piece titled "Lunar Rhapsody."*

Justin played several melodies for me on the piano and we chose one we both liked. Then he recorded a demo with the theremin. I remember my first reaction: I found the piece so sad, but a kind of sadness that's not of this world… a cosmic sadness! It was as if someone were singing millions of kilometres from Earth, and the echo of that lament reached me from the edge of the universe. The reactions from the executives, however, made me realise that the sound of the theremin most definitely isn't the most popular in the world. [*laughs*] But we stuck it out, and the studio eventually relented and agreed to let us use it in the film.

There's a beautiful version of the theme from Once Upon a Time in the West *by Sergio Leone played on the theremin. Listening to it made me wonder if Morricone used the instrument in the original version. It's intriguing.*

Yes, because the theremin has a vocal range. I love the instrument so much that I managed to include it briefly in *Babylon*.

Earlier you mentioned your intention to rely as much as possible on practical effects in First Man, *which meant using life-size replicas of the spacecraft used by astronauts for their missions. Is that why you hired production designer Nathan Crowley, one of Christopher Nolan's collaborators? I assume his experience on films like* Interstellar *and* Dunkirk *made him the ideal candidate.*

Absolutely. I really like the way space imagery was handled in *Interstellar*. It's one of the few films I find convincing in that regard. Even though I was aiming for a substantially different result in *First Man*, I needed an engineer capable of constructing spectacular sets without relying on digital effects, and Nathan Crowley fit the profile. He truly moved mountains.

What were the technical challenges?

With Nathan Crowley, Linus Sandgren and Paul Lambert overseeing the visual effects, we had meetings for months because everything had to be prepared before filming. We wanted to avoid using green screens and instead filmed the actors in replicas of the spacecraft or capsules, in front of a huge LED wall projecting space images. The shoot lasted fifty-eight days. We first filmed all the non-space scenes in documentary style, with a mobile camera and improvisation. That went relatively quickly. The second part of the shoot, dedicated to space sequences, took place entirely in the studio. We had planned to film twelve or thirteen shots on the first day, but at the end of the day, we had... absolutely nothing! I had never faced such a situation. It was immediately clear that the rest of the shoot was going to be complicated. Coordinating the capsule and the images displayed on the screen was important. Since the capsule was supposed to move, we also had to consider the position of the sun, which was simulated by mobile lighting. The capsule was so narrow that after putting on their astronaut suits, the actors could hardly move. It took an hour just to change their positions or that of the camera. It was a real nightmare. But we learned from our mistakes.

You used three film formats: 16mm for the scenes in the capsule, 35mm for Houston, and IMAX for the Moon. This technique, moving from one film format to another, was popularised by Christopher Nolan, but when it comes to his films – which are often beautiful, even spectacular – I don't see any good reason for it apart from aesthetic considerations. In First Man, *on the other hand, the shifts in format are coherent at narrative, aesthetic and scientific levels.*

I wanted the aesthetics of *First Man* to be unlike any other space film, where the images are generally uniformly clear and precise. We mixed formats and lenses, some of which had actually been used by NASA to film on the Moon. My visual references were the films shot by astronauts with 16mm cameras or recorded by cameras positioned on the capsule, and photographs taken by Aldrin and Armstrong with their Hasselblad cameras. Their training included photography courses, and although they weren't professional photographers, they got some really exceptional images. I was struck by the contrast between the less defined and grainy 16mm images and the great precision of the Hasselblad photographs. That's what inspired the transition from 16mm to IMAX, which I wanted to be as impactful as the shift from black-and-white to colour in *The Wizard of Oz*. I also had in mind a remark by Dave Scott[2] about the level of acuity of the astronauts on the Moon: they felt like they were in a lucid dream. Perhaps this was due to the incredible adrenaline rush they must have experienced, but also likely because of the absence of atmosphere or the clarity of the Moon's surface, which has no equivalent on Earth. It's as if they passed from one life to another. In fact, that's what one of the controllers says in the audio archives: "They've passed into another life that we can't follow." Of course, in the film, we do try to follow them…

For the making of his documentary Apollo 11, *released on the occasion of the fiftieth anniversary of man's first steps on the Moon, Todd Douglas Miller drew from the 279 reels of various formats preserved by the US National Archives, which had never been seen before. Did you look at this material during pre-production of* First Man?

No, but we did look at many other images that had never been distributed, which have been preserved in Huntsville, Alabama, where the spacecraft were manufactured – notably, large-format 65mm archive photographs of the launch of the Saturn V rocket. They served as a basis for our own images.

In addition to these visual archives, there are the 19,000 hours of audio archives from the Apollo mission, which NASA made public in 2018.

Whenever possible, we prioritised authentic audio archives in the film. During pre–production, I spent hours listening to recordings on YouTube. What's impressive is that sometimes life or death questions arise, but the astronauts never panic. The language of these archives is difficult for non-initiates to grasp, but there's a kind of magic to it, stemming from the quality of the audio, the Midwest accent of the astronauts, their self-control, and the jargon they use. It's as beautiful as a Bach cantata! And the fact that so much of it is difficult to understand makes the tapes even more fascinating.

A website has been created to relive, in real-time, the 102 hours, 45 minutes, and 42 seconds of the Apollo mission.[3]

It's fantastic – a combination of audio archives, camera images from inside or on the capsule, a map showing the altitude and movements of the rocket, and a transcription of exchanges between the astronauts and the control centre in Houston. It was invaluable for us in reconstructing the lunar landing. To go back to your question about the audio archives, let me add something that not a lot of people know, which is that since I wanted to film the journey to the Moon like a documentary, we made a point of ensuring the accuracy of the exchanges between the three astronauts and the control centre. We had transcripts, but they were fragmented. First, we had to identify the sections we wanted to recreate, then the missing parts. In order to do that, Josh Singer spoke with the actual NASA controllers.

When we began rehearsals, we quickly realised that each actor needed to know what to say if I decided, at any given moment, to film one controller over another, because I wanted complete freedom for each take and the ability to film in a continuous shot, so Josh wrote about twenty different scenarios specifically for the scenes set in the control centre. It was a lot of work. When we shot the scenes, every actor playing a controller had a microphone and their own unique version of the script. During editing, we had twenty-four audio sources – one per controller – which allowed us to select which ones we wanted to hear with the visuals. It's important to note that our extras weren't professional actors. We chose people who knew what to say or do in case of last-minute improvisation. Since we were filming in Atlanta, we brought together mainly civilian airport controllers and military base controllers. A few NASA controllers, Neil Armstrong's two sons and one of his grandsons also joined the cast. When we all rehearsed together for the first time, armed with scripts, it was like listening to an orchestra where each musician had brought a different score. Absolute chaos! Everyone had to find their place in the ensemble performance. It meant we had to rehearse the mission control sequences every weekend, since we were filming during the week.

We have talked about the music and the voices, but I would like to discuss more broadly the important role of sound in First Man. *In the opening sequence, Armstrong undergoes a test flight in the X-15 rocket plane. When the cockpit creaks in all directions, it sounds like the sinking of the Titanic. This ambience, combined with very tight shots of Armstrong's face and the windshield of the craft, intensifies the feeling of claustrophobia for the viewer.*

Most of the film takes on a subjective point of view. With a few exceptions, the viewer never sees what the astronaut is unable to see himself. For this reason, I wanted sound to play an even more significant role than usual, to enhance the three-dimensionality of the film and for the viewer to grasp the rudimentary aspect of the crafts the astronauts travelled in. When you look at the old American spacecrafts, and even more so the Soviet ones, they look more like Jules Verne's or Jacques Cousteau's submarines than spaceships. I wanted to do things differently from most space films and in this respect emphasise sound. My quest for realism also led me to show the journey into space as a descent into deep darkness. I was struck by the absence of stars in the photographs from the Apollo mission,[4] whereas the imagery from science-fiction cinema, starting with Kubrick's *2001* in 1968, is full of stars. The space in *First Man* is an absolute blackness that stretches into infinity, without any points of light – like being stuck in a cellar or a sealed coffin. It's mysterious and frightening. Total darkness and playing with noise and soundscapes are, in fact, two of the main ingredients of horror cinema. *First Man* sometimes borrows from that genre.

Ryan Gosling used an expression during pre-production, "the Moon and the kitchen sink," to illustrate the dichotomy of the story, which portrays a mythic journey while simultaneously seeking to demythologise it.

"The Moon and the kitchen sink" foregrounds the ordinariness of the daily life of these astronaut families, who were middle-class. That's what led us to film the everyday sequences kind of like home movies, to contrast them with the enormity of space exploration. Armstrong, despite being the hero who went into space, took out the trash and cleaned his pool. It reminded me of Homer's *Odyssey,* where trivial details about food or bodily functions punctuate Ulysses' voyage. If I have one regret, it's not pushing further to showcase this ordinariness in *First Man*.

The idea comes together beautifully in the shot of the fly walking on the rocket's dashboard while Armstrong is preparing for lift-off. We're in the context of an important mission, but we're watching this distracting insect. There's nothing more down-to-earth than that.

That's definitely one of my favourite shots in the film. [*laughs*]

Casting Ryan Gosling in the role of Neil Armstrong makes good sense, but what convinced you that Claire Foy, the British actress from The Crown, *would be convincing in the role of Janet, his wife?*

Initially, it seemed quite clear that we would cast an American, but my casting director, Francine Maisler, suggested Claire Foy, whom I didn't know, and initially rejected because she's English. But Claire's audition was extraordinary, and I changed my mind.

She embodies her character admirably – a blend of strength and fragility. She really is the revelation of the film.

She delivers a very beautiful, very sensitive portrayal. I never had the privilege of knowing Neil Armstrong, who passed away in 2012, but I did have the chance to meet his wife, and I became friends with their sons, Rick and Mark. Janet Armstrong is a remarkable, singular woman with a very distinctive voice. I listened to her recount her memories, which weren't necessarily tidy stories. I appreciated her frankness, which is characteristic of the Midwest. I fell in love with the place while I was location scouting, even though it's looked at with a certain snobbishness by people who live on the Atlantic and Pacific coasts. There's actually a derogatory expression for that part of America: "flyover country." And yet, the more time I spent there, the more I felt I was discovering authentic America, with its vast plains and cornfields, where the sky is bigger than anywhere else you've ever been and exudes a distinct American form of poetry. That's why more astronauts come from Ohio than from any other part of the United States. The first men to walk on the Moon could never have come from Los Angeles.

The supporting roles in First Man *are played by actors like Corey Stoll as an unsympathetic Buzz Aldrin, Lukas Haas as Michael Collins, and Jason Clarke as Ed White. White's wife is played by your own wife, Olivia Hamilton, who appears briefly in* La La Land *and has a supporting role in* Babylon. *Would you ever consider entrusting her with the lead role in one of your films?*

Sure, but it all depends on her. I didn't audition her for *Babylon* because I already knew she was perfect for the role, which is more significant than any I've previously entrusted her with. But she did have to audition for the role of Pat White in *First Man* because it was quite different from her usual repertoire. During pre-production, she met Pat's daughter Bonnie and they became friends. The White family's story is relatively unknown. We tend to forget that Ed White was the first American to perform an extravehicular activity, which was a big deal for the Gemini mission. He was one of NASA's heroes before the accident that killed him. It was important for us to meet the astronauts' families and interact with them, to understand more about their lives at that time. They all lived in the same neighbourhood, a sort of company town where everyone worked for NASA as astronauts, controllers and scientists. They were striving towards a collective mission, which I look at as a collective sacrifice, because there were tragedies. Children lost their fathers, women lost their husbands. NASA didn't quite know how to handle these situations. It wasn't the culture of the time to address the anxiety, pain and trauma that families experienced. Some were left behind, and we well know that these kinds of scars never fully heal. Yet the sense of pride these families feel is so strong, which is what makes the story so moving and unique.

In his biography, James Hansen recounts the 1964 fire at the Armstrong house which nearly took the life of their six-year-old son, Rick. You filmed this scene but decided not to include it. Why?[5]

In the screenplay, the house fire was presented as one of the Armstrong family's failures. Besides the fact that the loss of a house isn't equivalent to the loss of a human life, I realised early on in the editing process that the scene wasn't working – it didn't convey the intended shock effect to audiences, even though the part where Ryan Gosling watches the flames rising into the sky looked really good. The whole event seemed trivial in the grand scope of Armstrong's journey, and in a film like this, nothing should be depicted solely because it actually happened. I don't regret shooting the scene, as it allowed us to replicate the Armstrong house in Houston down to the square inch – which was pretty costly. The only reason we rebuilt it instead of using an existing house was that it needed to be burned to the ground.

The death of Neil and Janet Armstrong's daughter at the age of two from a malignant brain tumour is at the heart of First Man. *Immediately after the opening sequence of Armstrong's test flight, a sharp cut introduces a scene where we see young Karen undergoing radiation treatment. Then we see Neil taking care of her, caressing her curls, and as these scenes unfold, accompanied by Justin Hurwitz's guitar theme, we hear a metallic squeak. The following shot reveals that it's the sound of the pulley lowering Karen's coffin into her grave. It's heart-wrenching.*

I must say that... [*after a pause, he continues, with restrained emotion*] I didn't yet have a child when I made the film, and I don't know if I would be capable of making it today. At least, it would be more difficult for me. At that time, I had a relatively abstract understanding of Armstrong's grief, whereas Ryan Gosling and Josh Singer, both fathers, had a much more intimate connection to the scene. When I showed the screenplay to Ryan, I told him it was a film about failure, and Armstrong's journey was that of someone who moved from one loss to another: Karen, then Elliot, then Ed. But it was Ryan who rightly pointed out that the film was really about the loss of a child. That doesn't mean the other losses don't matter, it's just that each of them linked back to Neil's experience of Karen's death. He had no other option but to go along with it, because there was no fighting that tragedy. It reminds me of a beautiful moment in Kenneth Lonergan's *Manchester by the Sea*, where Casey Affleck's character, who accidentally caused the death of his children in a house fire years earlier, confides the depth of his sorrow to his nephew. "I can't beat it," he says. You can't overcome the heartache. It leaves an indelible mark. It took hearing Ryan's reaction to the screenplay for me to realise that this is what *First Man* is primarily about.

During pre-production, I thought a lot about the story of Orpheus and Eurydice, which is one of my favourites from Greek mythology. Orpheus can't live with the loss of the woman he loves, so he undertakes a journey into the realm of the dead to try to bring her back – a journey no other mortal has ever dared to make. The myth ends with the impossible return of Eurydice to the world of the living. It prompted a kind of revelation for me... I finally understood why I found the Moon so mysterious and poetic. It's because it's the land of the dead. Not just metaphorically, but also scientifically. It's a barren celestial body, devoid of apparent life, colourless. It looks like a cemetery in space. When you think about it, every physical law governing the universe makes the journey to the Moon almost impossible. That's why the launch of a rocket is so brutal. Astronauts are crossing a boundary that humans aren't supposed to cross. It's so incredible, so dangerous, not to mention there's nothing more powerful than the propulsion of a rocket into space – except for the atomic bomb, which is another barrier that mankind has so dramatically crossed. For me, Armstrong is a kind of modern-day Orpheus, embarking on a journey where no mortal has ever set foot, perhaps to symbolically reunite with the person he's lost. But, like Orpheus, he realises he can't bring anything back from his journey and can never truly heal from his grief. The first step of man on the Moon gave a certain hope to humanity, but it was a negative epiphany, one that for Armstrong was accompanied by the absence of hope that he might ever see his daughter again.

The end of the sequence on the Moon is based on the assumption that Neil Armstrong took something with him as a tribute to Karen and left it on the Moon. In his book, James Hansen writes: "What could have made the first Moon landing more meaningful 'for all mankind' than a father honoring the cherished memory of his beloved little girl, by taking a picture of the child, dead now over seven years (she would have been a ten-year-old), one of her toys, an article of her clothing, a lock of hair, her baby bracelet?"[6] It's this last option that you chose in the film. The disappearance of the bracelet into the shadow of the crater is an unforgettable, poignant image.

June, Neil's sister, had this idea that he might have left something belonging to Karen on the Moon. During the Apollo 16 mission, Charles Duke did actually leave a Polaroid of his family, and there's a photograph of this photo, which is really beautiful – just a regular American family, not even framed, left for eternity on the lunar surface. In Neil's case, the possibility that he might have taken Karen's birth bracelet with him sheds light on an interesting facet of his personality, which is that when talking with some of his closest colleagues and friends, people who had worked with him all their lives, it's surprising to discover that many didn't know he had a daughter. Others were aware that he had lost a child, but didn't think it had affected him much because he didn't talk about it. And yet his sister says it was the greatest tragedy of his life, one he never truly recovered from. It's a striking contradiction but easily explained: pouring out grief over the loss of a loved one wasn't the kind of thing that happened at NASA. Armstrong had been a test pilot and then an astronaut, two very dangerous jobs with a high risk of death. It was expected of him that he would control his emotions, but he was haunted by this loss. At a certain point during filming, I began to think of *First Man* as a story haunted by ghosts.

The loss of a child is what connects First Man *with Denis Villeneuve's* Arrival.

True, I hadn't thought about that.

I find it beautiful how both films, despite their differences, bring scientific exploration into the realm of the personal and intimate, with a rare sensitivity and without descending into melodrama.

Travelling through space, contemplating the possible existence of other life forms in the universe, dealing with grief – all are situations that bring us face to face with the question of an afterlife and the existence of God. It's also the subject of Andrei Tarkovsky's *Solaris.*

Which brings us back to the myth of Orpheus and Eurydice...

Exactly. Neil liked to tell his sons about the Moon landing from the Moon's perspective, not from Earth's. He would say that the astronauts arriving with their strange vehicles to conduct experiments looked like aliens. It was a science-fiction film in reverse. Tom Cross and I made extensive use of images of Neil wearing his helmet, visor down, his face invisible. He's quite an enigmatic character throughout the film, but once we get to the Moon, he takes on an almost non-human appearance and becomes a kind of extraterrestrial, or, from a more spiritual point of view, an angel or a ghost. Yet it's the first time we delve into his mind by showing his memories with Karen[7] – another paradox that appealed to me. The scene on the Moon is a bit of an anti-climax after the successful landing. The astronauts are safe, tension has dissipated, so now what is there to do? The moments that follow something momentous can be interesting. Once you've attained your goal, what happens next? I wanted this sequence to be simple and calm, with empty and wide-open images so that the audience can fill them with their own emotions.

Ultimately, isn't First Man *about a man trying to escape as far as possible from Earth rather than a man trying to reach the Moon?*

In a sense, yes. Neil was already "departed" when Karen died, and in the years that followed he channelled his efforts on pushing past boundaries that no one had ever crossed before. The film's epilogue raises a profound question: is it really possible to "return" from a journey like that? This is the essence of the scene where Neil and Janet reunite, separated by a large window, at the quarantine facility.

Neil Armstrong finds himself in the same position as the extraterrestrials in Arrival *and Janet now has to relearn how to communicate with him. But as always in your films, it's an open ending.*

It's an ambiguous moment of illusory hope, especially considering that Neil and Janet divorced two decades later.

And it's a bold ending for a film, because in the public's imagination, the Apollo 11 mission is regarded as having been a complete success. There's a stark contrast between this scene depicting the couple's melancholic reunion and the archival images that precede it of jubilant crowds celebrating the astronauts as heroes. Not only did you decide against reconstructing these moments of collective euphoria, you also opted for something quite radical: including raw, unaltered archival footage in its original form, which is very different from the trend of enhancing or beautifying archival material, like colourising black-and-white footage, cropping it, or even blurring the line between authentic archival and recreated images.

I chose to keep the imperfections because they immerse us in the viewing experiences of the time. These archival images served as a bridge between the Moon sequence, shot in IMAX, and the epilogue set in the quarantine zone, shot on 35mm. I also wanted to underscore the contrast between the crowd's excitement and Neil's solitude. The first step of man on the Moon is both the outcome of a collective effort, involving thousands of people on behalf of all humanity, and an individual one, that of a man who has forever remained the "first" in collective memory, even though he wasn't the sole member of the Apollo 11 mission. Isn't it ironic?

It certainly is. All these paradoxes add a layer of intrigue to the film. You manage to avoid excessive praise, and yet never fall into outright anti-patriotism. But despite that, there were various attempts to exploit and politicise the film. Some interpreted the fact that it doesn't show the astronauts planting the American flag on the Moon as a political message, and President Donald Trump more or less implicitly called for a boycott of First Man.[8] *Buzz Aldrin even tweeted pictures of the lunar landing with the hashtag #proudtobeAmerican. Was it really a big deal in the United States?*

It actually got pretty heated. From my perspective, the debate highlighted the divide between the East and West Coasts – including Hollywood – and the rest of the country. For years, long before Trump's arrival in the White House, a significant number of Americans felt that Hollywood and the media were looking down on them. And they're not entirely wrong because there's a definitely a sense of superiority among the elites, who often condescend to those who don't share their views on various subjects. Think about the flag, or guns, which are deeply rooted symbols in American culture but that which Hollywood often fails to grasp, sometimes even making fun of them. That partly explains the flag controversy in *First Man*. Ironically, it didn't start with the Trump-supporting media. It originated with a British media outlet linked to Hollywood, claiming that the "absence" of the flag in the Moon sequence was an anti-Trump symbol – as if everything has to carry a hidden message. The right wing caught wind of this rumour and it spread like wildfire. Most of the people fuelling the controversy hadn't even seen the film, and to make matters worse they thought we had completely omitted the flag, which isn't true. I have explained over and over again that there's no subliminal political message in *First Man*. I regret all the controversy, which really did surprise me. Maybe I'm naïve, although in hindsight I can understand what people who deeply respect the flag must have felt. I don't feel anger or frustration towards them, I just think that their frustration with Hollywood snobbery clouded their perception of the film.

Do you think that the underlying irony in First Man *might also have exacerbated feelings of hostility towards the film? The screenplay subtly sketches the historical backdrop of the space race, including unsettling contrasts, for example protests by African Americans who were opposed to the Apollo mission, and mention of Wernher von Braun, one of its instigators. The allusion is fleeting, but it still suggests that Americans needed the help of Nazis to get to the Moon.*

Absolutely. Just as in France, the context of the 1960s plays an important role in shaping cultural memories in the United States. When you think about it, two major threads come to mind. On one hand are the student protests against Vietnam, the struggles for civil rights, and Woodstock. On the other is the Apollo mission. These are the two poles of the same collective imagination. Today we have a highly idealised, almost psychedelic perception of man's first steps on the Moon. We forget that it was a government operation involving military technology and former Nazis. By the way, the Russians did the exact same thing. The Americans could have worked solely with the military, but they also enlisted civilian engineers. Why? Because they figured it was time to tackle an image problem: space exploration seemed to be the flip side of Vietnam. In their own way, both events were consequences of the Cold War.

The early 1960s were a continuation of the 1950s, with this illusory idea – existing mostly for white Americans – of a unified America rallied behind a single goal. Ironically, the closer we got to the Moon, the less support there was for the space programme. There was a spectacular surge at the time of the Apollo 11 mission, but a few months earlier, the majority of the country was against it, and the government turned a deaf ear. In other words, the nation was represented by a handful of people who, once their goal was achieved, had almost no support from the population. Things might have played out very differently a decade earlier, but by the late 1960s, the shadow of Vietnam loomed large. The increase in poverty and inequality, along with riots in cities and on campuses, made the idea of space conquest increasingly outdated and out of touch. The money, skills and lives spent on the race to the Moon could have been used for education, fighting poverty and inequalities – which were, in fact, the very demands of Ralph Abernathy, one of the leaders of the civil rights movement.

For others, space exploration seemed to hide militaristic motives. This brings us back to the infamous flag controversy, which dates back to that time. Some members of Congress thought it would be better to plant the United Nations flag on the Moon because they were worried that the American flag would be seen as a symbol of imperialism and aggression. Their opponents fired back, arguing, "This is ridiculous! This entire mission was paid for with public funds, and for that reason alone, Americans should have their flag on the Moon!" They got their way, but this decision was highly contested and became a major political issue. I think it's impossible to tell the story of the space race without being honest about the gaping divide that fractured the country. But that's the real challenge, because it's an event organised and supported by the establishment at the heart of a decade heavily influenced by anti-establishment sentiments.

Later criticism of the space programme veered into conspiracy theories, such as claims that humans never actually went to the Moon and that the Apollo mission was one big hoax staged by the Pentagon, with the help of Stanley Kubrick.

It all speaks to the fragile perception of space exploration. After the success of the Apollo 11 mission, enthusiasm quickly waned. Arthur C. Clarke's vision, shared by many at the time, that space conquest would mark the beginning of a new civilisation, was never realised – or only to a limited extent. Today, we hear that NASA plans to send a mission to the Moon by 2025. But we've been hearing that story for decades. Humans were able to go to the Moon at a time when computers didn't even exist, using technology that now fits entirely within a micrometre of this mobile phone [*he points to the thickness of his iPhone*]. The rocket used for the Apollo 11 mission was launched, essentially, with the power of a calculator. And all this without the support of the United Nations. It really was an achievement that hasn't been repeated since the early 1970s, despite so many technological advances. It's not a coincidence.

Personally, I admire the work done by NASA and the astronauts, but if I had been alive at the time, I'm sure I would have thought about how money for space conquest could have been better spent. In *First Man*, I even showcase a passage from an interview with Kurt Vonnegut in which he denounces the fact that so much money was spent on going to the Moon while the centre of New York was in such dire need of improvement. I couldn't understand it when a critic accused me of trying to discredit Vonnegut's point of view. On the contrary, I chose to incorporate that archival fragment because I'm sensitive to his arguments. The song by Gil Scott-Heron, "Whitey on the Moon,"[9] which I use somewhat anachronistically, seems to perfectly reflect the stakes of the debate.

You mentioned at the beginning of our discussion that First Man *was a commercial failure. I would tend to qualify that because, despite costing nearly $60 million, it grossed $145 million, of which just under $45 million came from the United States alone. Considering the film's theme, narrative approach and aesthetic choices, as well as the considerable risk it represented for you after the global success of* La La Land, *this "semi-failure" is somewhat relative. However, it's undeniable that the critical reception was lukewarm.*

First Man was judged too "traditional" by those hoping for a more radical film and too "radical" by those expecting something more conventional. So I only managed to displease everyone! [*laughs*] In the United States, the flag controversy didn't help matters, nor did the release date or the film's distribution work in our favour.[10] If most viewers had simply been able to appreciate the film for what it was, immersing themselves in the story, none of these explanations would have been necessary. For most of the public and critics, *First Man* was a disappointment. But I made a film that really mattered to me.

---

1. James R. Hansen, *First Man: The Life of Neil A. Armstrong* (Simon & Schuster, 2005).
2. After completing several spaceflights as part of the Gemini 8 and Apollo 9 missions, Dave Scott walked on the lunar surface as the commander of the Apollo 15 mission (July/August 1971). He served as a consultant on the set of several films related to space exploration, including Ron Howard's *Apollo 13* and Brian De Palma's *Mission to Mars*. He is portrayed in *First Man* by Christopher Abbott.
3. The website also allows you to experience the missions of Apollo 13 and Apollo 17 in real-time: https://apolloinrealtime.org.
4. This absence of stars in the photos taken on the Moon can be explained by the fact that the astronauts could only see Earth, the Sun and the Moon from their illuminated lunar module window. As for photos taken on the lunar surface, since it was illuminated by the Sun, the astronauts' cameras would have needed longer exposure times to capture the light of the stars.

5. The scene is a bonus feature on the Universal DVD/Blu-ray release of *First Man*.
6. Hansen, 380.
7. The images from these flashbacks were shot in 16mm and scaled up to match the IMAX format.
8. Laura Bradley, "Of Course Donald Trump Has an Opinion About *First Man*'s Dumb Flag Controversy," *Vanity Fair*, 5 September 2018. For a comprehensive overview of the issue, see Steve Rose, "If anyone can Maga, it is Nasa," *The Guardian*, 6 September 2018.
9. Scott-Heron's poem ["A rat done bit my sister Nell/(with Whitey on the moon)"] appears on his debut studio album, *Small Talk at 125th and Lenox* (1970).
10. The release date of *First Man* in the U.S. was 12 October 2018, a few months before the fiftieth anniversary of man's first trip to the Moon.

ANOTHER TEMPO
The Eddy

With The Eddy, *Netflix gave you the opportunity to make a mini-series. The story is set in a Parisian jazz club owned by Elliot Udo, played by André Holland, a renowned New York jazz pianist on the skids, as he tries to rescue the club from bankruptcy while dealing with various personal and emotional struggles. Each of the eight episodes focuses on a particular character. Was working in television one of your goals when you started making films?*

No, it wasn't something that particularly appealed to me. From my perspective, and regardless of how much I enjoyed watching television, I always felt there should be a clear distinction between TV and cinema. That's how I thought about it at the time. Ricky Gervais and Stephen Merchant's BBC sitcom *The Office* (2001-03) was, in my opinion, the best piece of television ever. I loved the lack of pretension and how it parodied the grand documentary tradition of the BBC. I was much less interested in dramatic series, and in general hadn't seen anything on television that could rival cinema. These days, I'm much more open-minded about the differences – or absence of them – between audiovisual forms.

The Eddy certainly attests to that. Originally, Glen Ballard came up with the idea of a series for which he composed a set of jazz songs and which he presented to director Alan Poul, who – knowing your early films and love for jazz – contacted you to develop the project. British playwright Jack Thorne later joined to write the script, somewhat reversing the usual process of starting with the story before composing the music.

That's right. Between the time we started discussing the project and filming it, a lot of time passed and we all went in different directions, before the process unfolded organically. When it came to the look and feel of the show, the same kinds of things that had inspired *Guy and Madeline* were important here too: Jean Rouch, concert films like *Jazz on a Summer's Day* and *Gimme Shelter*, and the CBS TV show *The Sound of Jazz*, where Billie Holliday and Lester Young, among others, performed "Fine and Mellow." I love the way their expressions and emotions were captured on film. I also wanted to reference the documentary tradition of Robert Drew, a direct cinema pioneer, and his films *Primary* and *Crisis*. The emergence of television in the early 1960s coincided with cinéma vérité, a connection that particularly interested me because I wanted to find an original style, different from big-screen cinema, which harked back to the 16mm documentary experiments I had done when I was a student.

I bought into the series format and the imposed framework, while also trying to go beyond it, which wasn't easy to do. Television that tries to pass itself off as cinema tends to annoy me, and I'm equally irritated by films shot in the style of bad TV movies, which give the impression of watching television-calibrated images on the big screen. It's even more noticeable in digital. I defined *The Eddy*'s aesthetics in response to that. I would even say that's what persuaded me to make the series. If Netflix had put restrictions on me from the start, I would have thrown in the towel. They did try to dissuade me from shooting in 16mm, but that was among the non-negotiable aspects, along with shooting handheld, the use of improvisation, and filming live music.

Netflix did allow you to shoot the first two episodes in 16mm, but the remaining six, directed by Houda Benyamina, Laïla Marrakchi and Alan Poul, were shot digitally.

I thought that was pretty stupid, and I still don't understand why they wanted it that way. The silly compromise made at the start was that I had permission to film in 16mm, but no one else did. I tried to persuade the Netflix executives, but since they didn't seem open to discussion, I thought the best strategy was to play along until they saw for themselves the stylistic mismatch between the first two episodes and the rest. When we did camera tests and they saw the stylistic inconsistencies, I took the opportunity to tell them, in a slightly sarcastic tone, "You know, you're absolutely right. I've noticed it too. But I've got the perfect solution. We've already got a workflow going for 16mm: the laboratory is ready, everything is set, and as you see, the tests my crew have done are really good. The image isn't as murky as you thought it would be. There's an obvious solution: we shoot all episodes in 16mm." "NO, NO, NO! IMPOSSIBLE!" was their response. They preferred to impose digital on the other three directors and multiply post-production steps to recreate the 16mm aesthetic, instead of just continuing to use 16mm, which would have been easier and much less costly.

I don't quite understand Netflix's argument. Was it a financial one?

No, because 16mm is relatively inexpensive. The real issue was the visual standards they had in mind. They were worried that audiences wouldn't understand that 16mm footage doesn't mean "lower quality" but is actually a distinct aesthetic choice. To convince them, I even organised a grading session with Linus Sandgren where I invited a technical team from Netflix, just to show them that 16mm resolution is equivalent to or even better than 4K, which makes sense because it's a chemical process translated into digital pixels for broadcast. When you watch images shot in 16mm, there's no loss of information, but no matter how compelling my arguments were, there was no room for dialogue because it clashed with how Netflix normally does things.

Looking back, though, I'm not sure the other directors were as enthusiastic about 16mm as I was. Most were used to digital, and it was important for each of them to do their own thing stylistically. There had to be overall unity, but in my mind *The Eddy* was supposed to resemble the omnibus films of the 1960s more than a traditional series, where each director aligns their style to the pilot episode. The battle to shoot the entire series in 16mm was mine, but not necessarily everyone else's, so I eventually gave up. The cinematographers for the other episodes, Julien Poupard and Marie Spencer, were good about handling Netflix's demands. They created a look that diverged from the digital texture of most TV. Maintaining visual consistency between episodes would have been easier if everyone had been using the same format, but the other filmmakers and technicians were resourceful and rose to the challenge.

How did you come to hire the two directors, Houda Benyamina and Laïla Marrakchi?

Houda Benyamina was top of my list, and after seeing her remarkable film *Divines*, I met her during the initial location scout in Paris. She's an extremely passionate and talented filmmaker, full of ideas and very proactive. We hit it off, and I can't have imagined a better partnership, which was important because our episodes followed one after the other and I needed to ensure a smooth handover, something I didn't have to do with Laïla or Alan. So I spent a lot of time with Houda. I asked for her opinion on the casting of my episodes, she asked for my input on the music in her episodes, and so on. We went location scouting a few times together because she knows Paris and the suburbs like the back of her hand, and she visited me on set when I was shooting. Houda became not only a collaborator but also an important source of inspiration and learning for me. Maybe I was the same for her, although I'm sure not to the same extent. I met Laïla Marrakchi a little later. The idea of hiring her came from the

French team. We arranged a meeting, and Houda, Alan and I quickly felt she was the right person for the job, but it was really with Houda that I had the closest working relationship.

The Eddy is a successful blend of your style and hers. The action unfolds in a diverse, working-class Paris, where graffiti and suburban issues aren't overshadowed. The club is located in the 12th arrondissement rather than Saint-Germain-des-Prés, seemingly to avoid picturesque imagery, unlike the dream epilogue of La La Land, *which reconstructs the Caveau de la Huchette.[1] Was that idea in the script?*

To be honest, I don't remember. I think so. I think that in one of the early drafts, the club was situated in central Paris, so the musicians travelled between the centre of the city and its outskirts, but we dropped that idea. One thing is certain: when Houda joined the project, it was already decided that the club wouldn't be in the Latin Quarter.

I read that Glen Ballard had assembled a band to play the songs even before the script was written. Does that mean the casting of the musicians was done well in advance?

Some were chosen at the start of the project, like pianist Randy Kerber and trumpet player Ludovic Louis, who had previously worked with Glen Ballard. Finding the other musicians – bassist Damián Nueva, drummer Lada Obradovic and saxophonist Jowee Omicil – took time, and was done as the script was being written. Sometimes we held auditions, sometimes Randy Kerber suggested a musician he knew. We recorded videos to judge their musical skill, how they handled dialogue and whether they could improvise. Since we wanted to film live music, we needed exceptional musicians who could convincingly act their parts while also playing at the level Glen expected of them. We met with some musicians who were good actors, but whose playing wasn't quite up to par, as the pieces they had to perform were quite challenging. I remember, for instance, that initially we chose someone else instead of double bassist Damián

Nueva. He was convincing as an actor and we thought he knew his instrument, but when rehearsals began, Glen and Randy quickly realised he wasn't as strong as they thought. They needed virtuosos. It wasn't about presence, just musical performance. Fortunately, Damián came along. He had that presence and was very musically talented. Of course, talent wasn't everything. It took months and months of rehearsals for the musicians to become a cohesive jazz band.

The Polish actress Joanna Kulig, who plays the singer Maja, had already showcased her vocal talent in Pawel Pawlikowski's Cold War. *However, André Holland isn't a musician.*

We wanted a real actor in the lead role. It was crucial to find him early enough so that he had time to learn the piano, even if we don't see him play much. André put a lot of effort into it. Joanna, who I first saw in *Cold War*, joined the project relatively late but still early enough to rehearse with the band. The fact that she could sing and act was crucial because, as with the musicians, we struggled to find an actress who excelled in both.

How did you come to cast Tahar Rahim and Leila Bekhti, who play Farid, the club owner, and Amira, his wife?

I liked Tahar Rahim in *A Prophet* and was eager to work with him, as well as with Leila Bekhti, who was also in Jacques Audiard's film. They're a couple in real life, and the idea of having them play a couple on screen, blending documentary and fiction, appealed to me. Moreover, the role of Farid needed to be played by a charismatic actor capable of embodying the opposite of Elliot, who is always negative. They make for an unconventional duo – funny in some aspects, a bit like two brothers constantly bickering while also deeply caring for each other.

Tahar Rahim sings and plays the trumpet very convincingly, thanks to his three months of preparation with Ludovic Louis. He plays the character with a mix of lightness and grace. Farid is sunny and cheerful but has a dark side that briefly surfaces in the first episode.

You mean the kitchen scene with Leila? I love that bit. I didn't give Tahar any specific instructions for the scene. He talks about his money problems, and when Leila suggests he ask his father for help, his entire demeanour suddenly changes and he becomes much more serious. It's very subtle: for a few seconds, you see in his eyes that something's off, but he quickly smiles again, teasing her. That's pure Tahar. I didn't need to cut around it in the edit – he did it all in a single shot. That's the mark of a great actor.

I like the physical characterisation of his character: the ponytail, tank top, e-cigarette.

The essence of the character came from Jack Thorne's script, but Tahar added the physical elements to express it authentically.

There's a lot of room for improvisation in the music scenes. What about the dialogue?

We also relied on improvisation, depending on the actors. With the musicians, who were non-professional performers, we almost exclusively used improvisation, on stage and in the dressing rooms, based on the broad ideas in the script. The rehearsal scene that turns into an argument in the second episode, for example, was mostly improvised. The camera had to react to the characters, and we were focused more on conveying the essence of the script than sticking strictly to the written dialogue. Allowing non-professional actors to express themselves in their own words works better than limiting them to the script. As the shooting progressed and they felt more comfortable in front of the camera, we directed them like traditional actors by slipping in specific lines. For scenes without music, with only the actors, we stuck closer to the script but sometimes still allowed room for improvisation. I did the same kind of thing on *Guy and Madeline*.

How long did the filming of your two episodes last?

Twenty-five days, working five days a week. After that, I moved on to editing, still in Paris, not far from the filming location, while Houda was shooting her own episodes.

Did you visit other directors on set or in the editing room?

No. I went back to Los Angeles after finishing the edit. They sent me episodes and I sometimes gave feedback, but more than anything I wanted each episode to reflect the vision of its creator.

Did you encounter any particular issues with sound?

We were filming under studio recording conditions. When the band played and the actors spoke, their dialogue was inaudible unless they were wearing small microphones which allowed us to hear some of what they were saying. The sound quality wasn't great, but it suited the documentary style of the show. For some dialogue, we had to ask the musicians to lower the volume or stop playing for a few moments. When we were mixing, we took pieces from other takes to create the illusion of simultaneous music and dialogue. So sometimes we cheated, but the goal was to do as little as possible to maintain the integrity of the live-recorded music on stage.

Even though you didn't write The Eddy, *one can't help but see it as a synthesis of the motifs and themes of your previous films. Elliot, for example, embodies the character traits and obsessions of your past characters. He is as emotionally unstable as the trumpet player in* Guy and Madeline. *Like Sebastian in* La La Land, *he is fixated on the jazz club he owns, investing himself to the detriment of his personal life. He is eternally dissatisfied and an ultra-perfectionist, to the extent of mistreating his musicians, sometimes almost as harshly as Fletcher in* Whiplash. *And, similar to Neil Armstrong in* First Man, *he is haunted by the death of his son a few years earlier, which led to his divorce.*

True… I hadn't thought about that. Unlike Andrew in *Whiplash*, who is focused on the future, Elliot is full of remorse and lives in the past. It's extraordinary how André Holland, one of the best actors I've had the privilege of working with, expresses all this melancholy simply through looks and facial expressions between dialogue. Every time I filmed him in close-up, something happened that wasn't in the script, like in the first episode, the way he flicks his cigarette outside the club after his conversation with Franck Levy. It's initially a very trivial gesture that reminds me, in the way he does it, of the character played by Ben Gazzara in John Cassavetes' *The Killing of a Chinese Bookie*. I see in Elliot the same blend of gallantry, elegance and relaxation, but also sadness and heaviness – classic and modern at the same time.

The scene that closes the first episode of The Eddy *is almost the opposite of the opening one. You immerse us in the club's universe with a stunning long take, giving the impression that the music and direction are unfolding in unison. The relationships between the main characters are outlined while Maja sings "Call Me When You Get There," which sets the musical tone of the series. The final sequence, however, is more fragmented, as you alternate between shots of the band performing the club's song with shots of Elliot and his daughter Julie sitting in the audience, with the initial energy giving way to melancholy. The tragic outcome of this first episode, with Farid's unexpected murder, is amplified.*

It wasn't quite as planned in my mind. Early in pre-production, The cinematographer Éric Gautier and I agreed that the opening sequence should be in one long shot, both to set the tone and have the viewer feel that the music was being performed live. We returned to shot/reverse shot for the epilogue because it was about establishing a silent dialogue between Elliot and the band.

The third episode, directed by Houda Benyamina, begins with footage of Farid filmed with an iPhone, which Amira watches after his disappearance. This moving scene inspires a somewhat tangential question: you often use the iPhone to record rehearsals with your actors or to plan complex camera movements, and you used it to make a short film, The Stunt Double, *paying homage to various genres, like slapstick, Westerns, musicals, spy films, that kind of thing. Do you potentially see the iPhone as a tool that can compete with professional cameras, similar to how Steven Soderbergh used it to shoot* Unsane *and* High Flying Bird?

The iPhone has its temporary usefulness, as demonstrated by Houda's use of it in *The Eddy*, but I wouldn't use it instead of a camera for filming a feature film. If I need a lighter camera, I prefer the Bolex 16 or 8mm cameras. For me, the iPhone remains a preparatory tool. In the case of *The Stunt Double*, I liked the vertical format because playing with constraints can be fun, but I definitely prefer the horizontal. It was just a small promotional film made as part of Apple's "Shot on iPhone" campaign. Nothing too serious.

If the opportunity arises in the future, would you work on another TV show?

I'm not sure. Maybe…Who knows?

What memories do you have of your first shoot in France?

It was great. Working conditions in Paris, with a small crew, were very pleasant. Collaborating with André brought me a lot of joy, as did working with Tahar, Leila, Joanna, Amandla Stenberg…

Could you see yourself returning to shoot a feature film there with an exclusively French cast?

Yes, I would like that. Believe it or not, I think about it a lot. It would be a nice change.

1. The Caveau de la Huchette jazz club, established in 1948 in Paris' 5th arrondissement, hosted numerous musicians and singers, including Sidney Bechet, Lionel Hampton, Art Blakey, Bill Coleman, Boris Vian and Léo Ferré, and has also been used as a setting in several films, including Marcel Carné's *Les Tricheurs* (1958).

IN SEARCH OF LOST TIME
Babylon

Watching Babylon *at the recent screening in Paris for Academy members was an unforgettable experience. Your opening speech really struck a chord. It was very emotional.*

Because it's a historic place: Studio 28, the first avant-garde cinema in Paris, where films like Luis Buñuel's *L'Âge d'or* and the Marx Brothers' comedies were first shown.

Since you were busy during the screening, answering questions from French journalists who had seen the film the day before,[1] you weren't there to hear the applause from the audience as the end credits rolled. These kinds of screenings usually give a good sense of what the audience is feeling, and in this case, despite the sustained applause, there was no standing ovation. Some people even left the room when the rattlesnake attacks Margot Robbie, or a little later when the masked man eats a live rat. Not the sort of thing you expect to see in a Damien Chazelle film.

True enough. It's a little different from what I usually do. [*laughs*]

Your films often take a long time to come together, with years of development before they are ready for audiences. Was this the case with Babylon?

Yes. The idea for the film goes back about fifteen years. I outlined a pitch that I didn't do much with for the next decade. Every time I finished a film, I continued researching, working on the narrative structure and fleshing out the characters at a fairly abstract level. During the filming of *First Man*, I knew the time had come to focus more seriously on *Babylon*, so once post-production was done, I started writing the screenplay.

Babylon *tells the story of the transition from silent cinema to the talkies, through a colourful array of characters: Manny Torres, an idealistic Mexican immigrant who dreams of working on a film set; Nellie LaRoy, a hedonistic and eccentric young American woman who wants to be a star; Jack Conrad, a fading movie star; Lady Fay Zhu, a lesbian Chinese actress; Sidney Palmer, a black jazz trumpet player; Elinor St. John, a gossip columnist; and George Munn, a depressed producer. The script, which spans a period of nearly ten years, is about 180 pages. You weren't worried about being too ambitious?*

As I was writing the screenplay, I realised this wasn't going to be a two-hour film. I wanted it to be a portrait of society, of Hollywood and Los Angeles from the mid-1920s to the early 1950s. The story needed the scope of films like Francis Ford Coppola's *The Godfather* and Sergio Leone's *Once Upon a Time in America* – epic-length films, over three hours, each with a unique rhythm and almost a genre unto themselves. I initially tried to restrain myself because I knew the longer the screenplay, the harder it would be to finance, but even with the best of intentions, I couldn't make it shorter. [*laughs*] The first draft was already nearly 180 pages. Considering that one page of screenplay equals roughly one minute of film – that's the usual ratio – it meant that *Babylon* would be a three-hour film. I started bending formatting rules by reducing margins or arranging dialogue into two columns. During pre-production, Bob Wagner, who was in charge of scheduling, came to me and said, "I'm curious about the actual length of your screenplay… If we eliminate all the formatting tricks, it must be close to 220 pages, right?" I replied, "No, you're kidding! 220 pages? Impossible!" But actually, of course, he was absolutely right.

Because filming was postponed due to the pandemic, it means you've spent nearly four years working on Babylon.

That's about right. By the end of 2018, after finishing the first draft of the screenplay, I started looking for money and, along with my producers – Marc Platt, Matthew Plouffe and Olivia Hamilton – reaching out to every major studio. Most of them turned us down, but fortunately we knew someone at Paramount who fought hard to convince the executives to back the project. At this point, Brad Pitt hadn't yet joined the cast, and the role of Nellie LaRoy was supposed to be played by Emma Stone. Brad wasn't officially associated with the project when we submitted the screenplay to Paramount. Pre-production for the film started between late 2019 and early 2020. In March 2020, we initiated hard prep – the final stage of pre-production involving the entire crew – but after two weeks everything came to a halt because of the first lockdown. The pandemic hiatus forced us to reshuffle. Emma became pregnant, which meant she had to drop out, so I sent the script to Margot Robbie, who agreed to replace her. It took us a year to pull a crew together, which was very different from our original setup. Filming originally planned for summer 2020 got pushed to summer 2021, and then post-production, starting in late 2021, lasted longer than expected.

The budget for Babylon *was $80 million dollars, making it your most expensive film to date.*

That's true, but it's still an average budget for a Hollywood film, lower than most recent big American productions, especially considering we spent close to $7 million just on Covid safety measures. There were reports in the press last fall that *Babylon* cost $100 million or more, but that's total guesswork. It simply means we managed to make people believe that what they see on screen is much more expensive than in reality. Have you followed the discussions about Christopher Nolan's upcoming film *Oppenheimer*? There's been a lot of talk about its budget being lower than most of his previous films. Do you know the amount?

I have no idea.

$100 million. And they talk about a "very tight" budget! We're hardly spending an exorbitant amount on *Babylon*.

It's even more remarkable considering you filmed it old school, on location with lots of extras and more than seven thousand costumes.

Exactly. That's why for me, the experience of making Babylon was similar to that of *Whiplash*. It's funny, because although I had a much bigger budget compared to my previous films, I felt like I was back in the old days, constantly having to run around, up against the clock, worrying about money. With *La La Land* and *First Man*, I had more breathing space, but with *Babylon*, it was as if I was trying to pay homage, in just seventy days, to epics like *Lawrence of Arabia* and *Apocalypse Now* – which took sixteen months to film! That was the insane part of this whole thing. *Babylon* is all about that grandeur, and we had to preserve its epic dimensions – the wild crowds crashing in from both sides of the screen, colossal sets, flashy costumes – but also had to keep the cash flow in check. The real challenge was figuring out how to find ways, in such a short time, of making audiences think that *Babylon* is a big-budget film.

Even though Brad Pitt and Margot Robbie don't share any scenes in Tarantino's Once Upon a Time… in Hollywood, *there might have been some concern that* Babylon *could feel repetitive because of the similar subject matter. But that's not the case. Was Pitt your first choice for the role of Jack Conrad?*

He was, but I didn't necessarily have him in mind when I was writing the script. Actually, I didn't think about any specific actor, except those that the character was based on – John Gilbert, Douglas Fairbanks, Karl Dane, Gary Cooper, Max Linder.[2] I suppose that to some extent I was dreaming of the 1960s Marcello Mastroianni in the role.

What was Brad Pitt's reaction after reading the script?

He liked it, but he had doubts about his ability to nail the character's "party animal" side. After several discussions, during which I described to him precisely what I was looking for, he got excited and eventually signed on. I told him I saw Jack Conrad as a mix between the 1920s John Gilbert, the 1960s Marcello Mastroianni, and the 1970s Jack Nicholson.

That ties back to what you were saying in our previous conversation about the blend of classical and modern that you identified in André Holland. It seems that this is something you often look for in your actors.

Exactly. Every now and then, I notice these subtle, almost fleeting gestures from my actors that feel like they belong to another era. It's like a quick glimpse into something beyond the present. I tend to want to unveil the essence hiding behind a role or a character. For example, I tried to resurrect in Jack Conrad the melancholy of Burt Lancaster's Prince Salina in *The Leopard*.

It's wonderful the way you manage to use both Brad Pitt's talent for comedy, which he brilliantly displayed in Tarantino's Inglourious Basterds *and the Coen Brothers'* Burn After Reading, *and his melancholic side, which takes over in the final part of* Babylon, *leading to his suicide. I don't ever recall seeing him use these two sides in the same film.*

The role was somewhat written that way, but we pushed things even further when Brad arrived. As you say, he's an actor capable of shifting from slapstick comedy in the style of Peter Sellers – who I adore! – to a mix of fragility, tenderness and softness. He and I talked about this. Jack Conrad is an old school gentleman who isn't going to survive the era of silent cinema. In a way, he goes down with the ship, but with a certain... [*searching for the word in French*]

...panache?

Yes, panache. His final suicide isn't an act of despair: he accepts death with inevitability and elegance – the same elegance he maintains when drunk in the first part of the film.

Margot Robbie, whom I found rather transparent in Once Upon a Time in... Hollywood, *delivers a memorable performance in* Babylon. *She's funny and touching, vulgar and sophisticated, volcanic and sensitive. How did you direct her?*

I was surprised at how much Margot got into the role. When we sent her the script, we were in a tough spot because we had just lost Emma and there were lots of financial and scheduling issues to deal with. I was hoping Margot would agree to be in the movie, not only because we didn't have many other options, but also because her name would give the studio extra assurance. The stakes were pretty high. After reading the script, Margot was ready to audition for the role, but I wanted to offer her the part then and there. What was so fantastic was that I could sense she had the drive and ambition that perfectly matched the character, and because of that, directing her was relatively easy. She really is very talented – capable of amazing things on set. Since her role wasn't very subtle, what I mainly did was encourage her to push her boundaries, even get rid of the idea of limits altogether. I wanted her to express that wild, uncontrollable animal energy that defines the character. The risk was that she might lose some of her humanity, but Margot was quite naturally able to keep it in check, and with a lot of sensitivity too.

You chose Diego Calva to act opposite her – a relatively unknown young Mexican actor, whom you auditioned over Zoom.

I saw a photograph of Diego Calva and thought, "This guy has the face of a poet!" It was a gut response. I had no idea if he could act. He was living in Mexico, so I suggested that we talk over Zoom, which we did a few times until I invited him to do a "chemistry read," again over Zoom, first with Emma Stone, then with Margot Robbie when she took over from Emma. I hadn't decided anything at this stage – it was just to see the two of them together. To be honest, I couldn't picture Diego as Manny Torres, but Olivia disagreed and insisted he was perfect for the role. She tried to convince me, but I continued auditioning. I felt Diego was at a disadvantage because of his very limited experience. He went to film school to become a director and started acting in his friends' films without ever learning about acting, and his credits consisted of a handful of small independent films, all shot in Mexico. Plus, he had never set foot in the United States and spoke very little English. I've always liked working with non-professionals, but in this case I thought it was risky to entrust the role of Manny to Diego, especially in a film that required such a high level of technical complexity. This sparked heated debates between Olivia and me, and I ended up choosing another actor.

Several months passed, and after the filming was postponed due to the pandemic, a new scheduling issue arose: the actor I had chosen for the role of Manny had to start filming a series, and it was impossible to sync his schedule with ours. Olivia used the opportunity to bring Diego back into the mix. "We'll bring him to Los Angeles," she said, very convincingly, which became possible because the Covid travel restrictions had been lifted. Despite my telling her it was a waste of time, that I had already made my decision and it was final, she stuck to her guns. So we summoned Diego, along with two or three other actors, to read with Margot Robbie, in our garden. Unbeknownst to me, Olivia had given Diego specific clothes and styled his hair, which completely transformed him. He had gone from his skateboarder look to a character straight out of a Visconti or Coppola film. He looked like a young Al Pacino! His face, the way he looked and how he carried himself – it all seemed timeless. I asked him to read a scene with Margot, and as I filmed with my iPhone, what every filmmaker hopes for during an audition happened: a rare, magical connection between the two actors. Margot was a star, Diego was just a beginner, but they were bouncing lines back and forth like equals. I thought, "He's the one. He's Manny."

Because Diego had come out of nowhere, and there was no hiding his thick accent, we then had to convince the studio. [*laughs*] We showed his auditions to Paramount executives, who eventually decided to take a chance. But because of Diego's lack of experience, and considering that we had only a limited time to shoot, I decided to rehearse all his scenes in advance. He came to Los Angeles for some intense rehearsal sessions with a small group. Olivia played opposite him, performing all the other roles, and I filmed them with my iPhone. Then I edited the sequences on my computer with Justin's music, which allowed me to keep track of how Diego was doing. Manny is a character who undergoes an initiatory journey and gradually becomes an adult, so it was crucial to believe in his development. The film shot on my iPhone allowed me to detect any potential problems in Diego's performance as well as in the dialogue, which sometimes led me to make changes in the script. I could tell that Diego had fully embraced Manny and would be ready to give his all during the actual filming.

The characters in your films typically follow an upward trajectory. Despite facing obstacles, they tend to succeed, but only after having sacrificed something. Manny, on the contrary, despite moments of glory, sinks deeper into the depths of Hollywood as the story progresses, until the sequence in the bunker, which feels like he's descending into the circles of hell. "Abandon all hope, ye who enter here," reads the beginning of Canto III of Dante's Divine Comedy. *It could be a warning from* Babylon, *which is about lost illusions.*

When Manny manages to elude hell by escaping the bunker, he's lost most of his illusions but still carries the flame of his love for Nellie. When she goes, there's nothing left for him. He survives, unlike most of the characters in the film, but a part of himself has died, and he isn't the same man who returns to Los Angeles in the epilogue. If I had to sum up the movie in one sentence, I would say that *Babylon* is about Manny losing his innocence just as much as it is about Hollywood losing its soul.

According to some sources, Tobey Maguire, who plays the enigmatic James McKay, was initially cast as Charlie Chaplin. Can you confirm this?

No, that was never the case. It's a strange rumour from who knows where that spread on the internet while we were filming. Chaplin was never a character in the screenplay. James McKay is completely fictional.

I thought he was inspired by a gambler of the same name, who founded the Cal-Neva Lodge in the early 1920s.[3]

Really? What a coincidence! Unless it was an unconscious thing? I might have come across that name early on in my research. Maybe it lodged itself in some corner of my mind and resurfaced when I was writing. But I have no recollection of it. [*laughs*] What is true, however, is that he's inspired by the microcosm of Cal-Neva, which was tucked away in a sort of no man's land between California and Nevada, and wasn't under the jurisdiction of either state. This was before Las Vegas had been built. When gambling went underground, anyone who made their living from it sought refuge in Cal-Neva. It was best to steer clear of the kind of shady characters you would run into there. They operated on the fringes of

Hollywood and sometimes got mixed up in racketeering or murder, as seems to have been the case with the death of Thelma Todd. She was an actress who began working in the mid-1920s and had a decent career for a few years, until she turned up dead in her car. The official investigation said it was a carbon monoxide suicide, but because of her ties to the underworld, the police suspected the infamous gangster "Lucky Luciano" was involved.

With a few exceptions, like producer Irving Thalberg and press tycoon William Randolph Hearst, most of the characters in Babylon *are fictitious, which allows you a certain poetic license.*

Yes, I wanted to keep a certain distance. The film draws from reality but for the most part is fiction. However, most characters are inspired by real actors, actresses or personalities of the era. Nellie LaRoy's journey is more or less modelled after Clara Bow's; Manny is a combination of René Cardona and Enrique Vallejo; Lady Fay Zhu is a fictionalised Anna May Wong; director Ruth Adler bears some resemblance to Dorothy Arzner; and director Otto von Strassberger is inspired by Erich von Stroheim. Trumpet player Sidney Palmer is a mix of musicians who played in Central Avenue clubs, like Curtis Mosby or Sonny Clay, who had some small roles in early talkies.

Is his name a tribute to Jason Palmer?

Yes, and his first name to Sidney Bechet.

We haven't yet talked about the title: Babylon.

I love the mythical connotation. It evokes a once grand civilisation, now in decline.

Apart from ancient Babylon, the allusion is to symbolic Babylon in the revelations of Saint John, the "great prostitute" engaged in all sorts of abominations. The prologue in particular shows

Hollywood as a modern-day Sodom and Gomorrah. You also draw on anecdotes from Kenneth Anger's book Hollywood Babylon, *which is full of some of the most scandalous stories in Hollywood history.*

The sordidness of that book, which is like something out of a tabloid, as well as Kenneth Anger's literary technique, were big inspirations. Hollywood's nickname at the time was "the modern Babylon." Groups campaigning against "immorality" wanted to rein in its excesses. A few incidents made headlines, which led to an intensified moral scrutiny, culminating in the enforcement of the Hays Code from 1934 – the formalisation of a process that had begun in the 1920s. As well as the shift from silent to sound films, I wanted to show the transition from a world of absolute lawlessness to a highly regulated one. I really wanted to just crack open the illusion, put about by the studios, that Hollywood was squeaky clean and tightly regulated.

You show the relative diversity and open-mindedness in Hollywood during the silent era – a female director, a lesbian actress, a mix of minorities – but Babylon *never becomes an ideological statement. You don't shy away from Nellie and Lady Fay Zhu's relationship, but you don't dwell on it either. Nellie's bisexuality isn't a focal point of the story. This is all very different from Ryan Murphy's series* Hollywood, *which takes a revisionist approach to history: imagining what the industry would have been if, in the late 1940s, studios had given leading roles to black actors and homosexuals could have openly shown affection at the Oscars.*

I wanted to be honest by explaining that Hollywood became much less diverse after sound came in, until the 1960s or 70s – but without turning it into an ideological statement. We truly went from one extreme to the other. You can be nostalgic for the kind of freedom the crew of a silent film had, but it was the Wild West, where anything could happen – for better or worse. The restrictions that followed did a lot for safety on film sets, notably preventing accidents and protecting workers' rights through unions. But it also meant significantly less freedom, diversity and spontaneity. That's also the story of the film: a society undergoing a radical transformation.

Babylon *reflects one of the major themes of your work, as our conversations have highlighted: a love of paradox. The film continually shifts from the trivial to the graceful, from excess to subtlety. The opening and epilogue embody this dichotomy. The film begins with a scene where an elephant copiously defecates into the camera and concludes three hours later with Manny's tears as he sits in a cinema that is screening* Singin' in the Rain, *one of the great moments in film history. It couldn't be more diametrically opposed.*

I'm fascinating by the idea of paradox. The entire transitional period between silent and sound cinema was fundamentally paradoxical. On the one hand, Hollywood was never more debauched than during this period, but on the other, it produced the most angelic and transcendent images in the entire history of cinema. When I was a teenager, I found it hard to perceive stars like Greta Garbo or Louise Brooks as real people. In my mind, they were sublime apparitions, sacred icons. And yet, it goes without saying that they were made of flesh and blood, which also meant sweat, crap and sexual fluid.

When you read anecdotes about actors from the 1920s and '30s, you're struck by just how depraved they were with drugs, alcohol, orgies… Hollywood was simultaneously high and low, sublime and obscene, beautiful and ugly, noble and kitsch. I imagined it as a kind of refinery where absurd and disgusting, tragic and comedic, shocking, even stupid ingredients were mixed to create something that didn't seem to have been made by human hands but by a divine power, as if it had fallen from the heavens. That's the effect that silent cinema had: a close-up of Lillian Gish in a Griffith film is something absolutely pure and celestial, even though the entire process leading to its creation was the exact opposite.

What you're saying reminds me of the end of the battle sequence in the first part of Babylon. *Jack Conrad, who has spent the day drinking, has to shoot a love scene with an actress. He belches, almost vomits, but then, just as the sun is setting, in front of the camera he passionately kisses his partner – and a butterfly delicately lands on his shoulder. It's outrageously kitsch.*

Yes, and we intentionally exaggerated it. It brings to mind Umberto Eco's famous line about clichés.

Ever since Guy and Madeline, *you have presented yourself as a filmmaker of human bodies, following Cassavetes' notion that "characters must not come from a story or plot, but… the story should be secreted by the characters."*[4] *Bodily expressions and movement have a central place in your work. You often use close-up shots to depict the body at work and in the act of creation, or bodies drawn together, all within the framework of an idealised sense of romance. But with* Babylon, *for the first time, you emphasise all things carnal, the sexual and organic power of bodies, drawing inspiration from Paul Verhoeven's work. The opening scene of the film can be seen, in some way, as the* Eyes Wide Shut *orgy reimagined by the Verhoeven of* Showgirls.

My primary reference for that scene was Fellini. The noisy, crazy energy, with the music and circus-like atmosphere – it's inspired by *La dolce vita* and *8½*, which I watched over and over again and actually screened for the crew during pre-production. There's also the party scene in *I Vitelloni*, which I think Paul Thomas Anderson might be referencing in *Phantom Thread*. The whole carnival atmosphere comes from Fellini, including his later films like *The Clowns*. Of course, *Eyes Wide Shut* does come to mind, but more for the intimate sexual sequences, like the scene in the bedroom with Orville and the girl.

It's a direct reference to the tragic death of actress Virginia Rappe, following the party thrown by actor Roscoe "Fatty"

Arbuckle in a San Francisco hotel,⁵ which is represented in the film with a "golden shower" scene. Considering the kind of controversies we've seen, like the one around First Man, *I wouldn't be surprised if some left-leaning American media outlets interpret it as a nod to rumours about Donald Trump.⁶* [*laughs*]

I actually had the very same thought, but it's definitely an allusion to Fatty, not Trump.

Paul Verhoeven said that a film like Showgirls *would be impossible to make in Hollywood today because it's been overrun by a kind of "new puritanism."⁷* Babylon *tends to suggest the opposite. Brad Pitt said that on day one of filming the orgy sequence he was initially shocked to see so much nudity, but as time went by it felt like just a regular day at work. Did you face any particular pressure?*

None. I was prepared for difficulties with the MPA [Motion Picture Association], but it went rather smoothly. Actually, the only scene that caused trouble was the golden shower one. We had to make a few cuts, very minor ones, to get an R rating. The studio people were very supportive, but everything was already in the script, so there was nothing they were unaware of. I was much more concerned when I first handed the script to the studio because describing acts of violence or sexual nature on a page is riskier. You can't tell if they'll be filmed in close-up or if the camera will linger on them – that kind of thing.

Babylon *is filled with urine, semen, faeces and vomit. Producer George Munn gets his head stuck in a toilet seat and Nellie pukes in public at a fancy reception.*

I liked the idea of incorporating all that in an Oscar-bait film, a long, epic costume drama set in old Hollywood, when it's usually the kind of thing found in films that are deemed – wrongly, actually – as about as far from "high art" as can be. I'm talking about the Hollywood tradition of broad comedies, like *National Lampoon's Animal House*, *There's Something About Mary*, *Harold & Kumar*, *Old School* and *The Hangover*, which aren't usually associated with serious *auteurs* and good taste. By blending these two extremes, it's as if refined filmmakers like David Lean and Luchino Visconti incorporated crude humour and scatological characters into their films. These things seem contradictory from today's perspective, but if you go through the history of art, they absolutely weren't. Rabelais, Chaucer and Brueghel were all extremely vulgar. Even though society today seems more open and evolved, it's really wildly puritanical. I agree with Verhoeven on this. We have no problem watching the most brutal violence, but when it comes to breasts, vomit or excrement, it's no longer cinema – it's obscene and offensive. I wanted to draw attention to this, not to shock gratuitously, but to remind people that in its beginnings, cinema was a vulgar art.

Some people felt that film could be elevated to the level of Michelangelo or Leonardo, making it an equal of painting and theatre, and as a cinephile, I'm certain they succeeded. A close-up of Renée Falconetti in *The Passion of Joan of Arc* or Louise Brooks in *Pandora's Box* is as beautiful as a sculpture by Michelangelo, a portrait by Leonardo, or a sonata by Beethoven. Cinema is no exception: most arts were born in the gutter and strove for something better. You see it with jazz too. It used to be seen as noisy, raucous and downright dirty, but these days you can catch jazz performances at fancy Carnegie Hall. And the same thing goes for novels. Back in the day, they were considered something for "common folk" because they didn't have the highbrow status of tragedy, theatre or poetry.

There is also photography, which Baudelaire considered – at best – the "very humble servant" of the arts. I've always been struck by the contrast between the poetry of Chaplin's great films and the vulgarity of his early shorts.

Chaplin's Tramp was unsympathetic, angry and boorish – which is why the Surrealists liked him.

They didn't like the sentimentality of The Kid. *The Tramp they appreciated was more primitive, precisely because he embodied disorder.*

Yes – disorder, madness, frenzy! This is what I claim for *Babylon*, very much part of the spirit of the Roaring Twenties. There was a whole series of films called the Cokey Comedies because they were inspired by cocaine. The Keystone Cops, for example, running around like ants or driving like crazy in their cars. There's an absolutely fascinating element of delirium in those wild comedies. There were a lot of drugs going around in Hollywood, and while it's not fair to generalise, because many filmmakers never touched them, it certainly feels like some films of that period were made under the influence of psychotropic substances. I wanted *Babylon* to have the same effect.

Doesn't the primitive energy of Babylon *also come from the films of William Wellman?*

It's interesting that you mention Wellman because he's a major filmmaker from the transition of the late silent era to the early talkies. All his films, from *Wings* to *The Public Enemy*, made an impression on me.

His pre-Code films are striking, punchy, with a real in-your-face aesthetic. Night Nurse, *for example, opens with a sequence where the camera is inside an ambulance on a wild race to the hospital.*

We've lost that frenetic energy, the kind of thing you can also find in the avant-garde of the 1920s and '30s. I tend to think that "mainstream" filmmakers like Wellman, Mamoulian and Milestone, who were making pretty daring stuff, and avant-garde filmmakers like Dudley Murphy, were part of the same creative melting pot, where the vulgar merged with the artistic.

You compared the rhythm of Babylon *to that of a roller coaster. It feels like you were looking for an equivalent of the moment in* Singin' in the Rain *where Donald O'Connor performs "Make 'Em Laugh". There's a kind of wild, all-out commitment in that scene, which was largely improvised. With* Babylon, *it feels like you were doing the same kind of thing: pushing things further and further, to the point of exhaustion.*

The funny thing is that "Make 'Em Laugh" is the *Singin' in the Rain* number most rooted in silent film slapstick. I've always liked the idea of pushing things beyond the limit. I don't know how to find the right words to express it. It's kind of comparable to what Kubrick said when asked why he did so many takes. Even if the seventh or eighth take seemed perfect, he kept going, again and again, until the performers were so tired that they had lost some control over their performance, at which point new things would emerge in their acting. There's an equivalent to this method when a filmmaker uses repetition, the same thing over and over, in a single scene. Do you see what I mean?

Like in the bit in Babylon *where Nellie has to do the same thing again and again because of technical problems with the sound?*

Exactly! There's a similar scene in *Bridesmaids* when Anne and Helen have a speech duel to compete to be Lillian's best friend, who has chosen them both as bridesmaids for her wedding. After the first exchange you think you've got the joke, but they do it again and again, to the point where the scene isn't even comical anymore. It's provocative because there's a risk of going too far, doing the same joke too many times, or one time too many – and then it goes even further. But, of course, it works wonderfully. What would be, in a normal comedy, a completely banal scene becomes a completely brilliant, even iconic, moment. Along the same lines, I could mention the scene from *Monty Python's The Meaning of Life* where Mr. Creosote vomits uncontrollably in the fancy restaurant. It goes on and on and on… It's messy, it's disgusting, but it's brilliantly funny. There's a surreal aspect to it, where disorder disrupts and fragments any cinematic norms. But I'm sure that some would find the two examples I've just mentioned excessive because they go against what's considered good taste. I knew I wouldn't please everyone if I did the same kind of thing in *Babylon*. It was a risk I weighed. You might even say it was the whole point of the film.

The music, which in Babylon *is a full-fledged "character" in its own right, seems to me to stem from a similar intention: it deviates quite radically from the idea we might have of jazz from the 1920s. Was this your idea or Justin's?*

I was convinced, from the start, that we needed to steer clear of musical stereotypes. The same goes for dance: I told Mandy Moore that I especially didn't want anyone to do the Charleston. We discussed this a lot with Justin, who began doing his own research, which led him to rock, dance, electro-dance. Every time he found new sounds, he would send them to me, and I did the same. It took us months of work to define *Babylon*'s sonic identity.

There are also numerous references from the classical repertoire: Mussorgsky's "Night on Bald Mountain" is used for the scene of the medieval battle filming. The piece titled "Morning" quotes the opening bars of Schubert's Piano Trio No. 2 used by Kubrick in Barry Lyndon*. The musical progression of another piece, "Hearst Party", evokes Ravel's "Boléro", not to mention the opera tunes that Jack Conrad listens to. Was this all part of enhancing the contrasting and diverse aspects of the film?*

No, I don't think it was a conscious idea on my part – they're simply pieces of music that I love and felt were appropriate to illustrate certain passages in the film. Jack's love for opera, however, was a deliberate comment on his inferiority complex, as he tries to appear as a "serious artist" practising a "noble art." The use of classical music elsewhere in the film ended up echoing this idea, which wasn't originally planned.

I think I spotted Justin conducting the orchestra in the grand sequence at Kinoscope Studios. Was that him?

Yes, you've got a keen eye!

Are you also there among the extras?

Not on screen, although you can hear my voice, along with my editor Tom's, in the scene where Nellie overhears two guys gossiping about her behind the toilet door. I also play the character of Donny, laughing off-screen in the camera rental shop, and I did some of the voices in the crowd scenes where the audience laughs at Jack's film and fans chase Nellie in New York.

How would you describe Babylon's *overall structure?*

I conceived it as a succession of parties. Some are literal, like the orgy at the beginning, or the poolside meeting. Others are gatherings of characters that I choreographed as if they were at a party. These scenes build to a crescendo, and once the audience is caught up in the whirlwind, I thought it would be interesting to pause the action with a moment of vision, lucidity or calm before plunging back into chaos. It's a bit like someone suddenly turning off the music or switching to classical music in the middle of a deafening party.

That comparison reminds me of how abrupt the shifts in tone are in Babylon. *I was struck by the starkness with which you transition from one scene to another. It's as if sometimes the film was cut with a chainsaw, for example the horrific scene in the tunnel, which ends in blood and screams, with an abrupt cut to a jazz orchestra playing.*

The entire premise of the film is based on the idea of moving from comedy to tragedy, which was also there in *La La Land*. As I researched, I wanted to push it further because the things I was reading seemed to connect two extreme poles: the slapstick comedy of the Marx Brothers, Peter Sellers and

Monty Python, and the pure horror of films like Pasolini's
Salò, or the 120 Days of Sodom. I stacked sequences one on
top of the other, each with very pronounced contrasts and
alternating genres – as if *Babylon* were several films in one.

Babylon *serves as both a synthesis and development of a
subgenre: stories set behind the scenes in Hollywood, like*
Singin' in the Rain, Sunset Boulevard, Barton Fink *and*
Mulholland Drive. *But there are so many references in the
film that it becomes a kaleidoscope of aesthetics, which some
audiences may find too fragmented.*

At one point while I was working on the screenplay, I asked
one of the producers, "Do you think I should cut this or
that character? Should I tone it down?" He put his finger on
something so important, which is that the whole point of the
film is how overflowing and excessive it is. In other words,
the main character of *Babylon* isn't a black trumpet player
or a Mexican immigrant chasing success, or a fading silent
film star or a girl from humble beginnings who skyrockets
to stardom. The story is of a particular moment in time and
space toward which all these protagonists – these archetypes
– converge. We've heard the stories of Rudolph Valentino,
John Gilbert and Clara Bow a thousand times, to the point
that they've become pieces of old Hollywood mythology.
What interested me was how to bring them all together in that
pivotal moment when silent cinema became the talkies, which
at the time was earth-shattering. Rather than holding back,
I pushed things as far as possible, into excess, culminating
in the final explosion where the film reduces itself to the
essential components of cinema: colour, light and sound.

*There's a lot to be said about the magnificent ending, which
on screen is somewhat different from how it's written in the
script. Years after leaving Hollywood, Manny – who now lives
in New York and is married with a child – goes into a cinema
and watches* Singin' in the Rain. *The audience is laughing, but
he is caught in a whirlwind of conflicting emotions, and begins
to cry because the film reminds him of events he experienced*

two decades earlier. The script reads: "His tears fading, his still-watery eyes turning from the audience around him and looking once again onto the screen. The anger has gone now, and the sorrow with it. What remains instead, glistening through the residual moisture in those eyes, is some strange alchemy – of heartbreak, joy, regret, pride, sheer incredulity at the madness of it all – and finally, gratitude... He was a part of something bigger." But in the film, just before this final shot of Manny's face, you integrate a firework display of images drawn from some of the most iconic works in cinema history: from Georges Méliès' A Trip to the Moon *to James Cameron's* Avatar, *via Luis Buñuel's* Un Chien Andalou, *Alfred Hitchcock's* Psycho *and Griffith's Babylonian sets from* Intolerance. *This psychedelic montage ends up looking like a Stan Brakhage film, with abstract images evoking the chemical colourisation of a film, following by its editing.*

I wanted to end *Babylon* with this ultimate paradox: Manny crying while watching *Singin' in the Rain*, the musical that most embodies the joy of living. He has to reconcile the conflict between the beauty he sees on screen and the painful memories it stirs up. It's like memory colliding with art, which is heightened by cinema – the synthesis of all arts – more than any other form. When we were editing, this sequence, as written in the script, felt a little too constrained to me, because the whole philosophy of the film was about breaking down boundaries. So I thought about how I might be able to push this mix of emotion and uncertainty that grips Manny even further, and that's when I had the idea of including this frantic montage of images from cinema history. The abstract shots at the very end were originally filmed for a sequence for the first part of *Babylon*, showing the different stages of film editing. I had put them aside and ended up using them in the epilogue. It was the only way to end the film: to return one last time to these ideas of breaking through, of overflow, rupture and shock – but giving them new form.

It's like you merged the sequence where Bowman enters the fourth dimension in 2001: A Space Odyssey *with the final explosion of Zabriskie Point. Manny realises he's a tiny speck of stardust in the vast cinema galaxy.*

Remember what journalist Elinor St. John tells Jack Conrad when he confronts her about the negative article she wrote about him: "It's bigger than you." Regardless of the mark an actor or director leaves on cinema history, they're ultimately just a small part of this monumental edifice that transcends them.

To conclude, let's talk about Nellie's tragic end. She disappears into the night – just like she emerges from the darkness at the beginning of the film – and Manny never sees her again. But one detail in the film, absent from the script, stands out: after the brief montage of archive footage showing the evolution of Los Angeles, and just before the epilogue set in 1952, a small newspaper article reports Nellie's death at the age of thirty-four. This detail reinforces the symbolism of the scene where she literally plunges into darkness. The shooting star that splashed across the screen has faded into anonymity and disappeared into oblivion.

That's interesting. I went back and forth on this detail which, as you say, isn't in the script. When we screened the film for the very first time, I heard people say they expected Nellie to reappear in the 1952 epilogue. The ellipsis led them to think that the two characters would be reunited, like Sebastian and Mia in *La La Land*. It seemed to me that Nellie's disappearance into the darkness of the night signified her death pretty clearly, but I figured I should take audience feedback into account. It offered a new possibility: highlighting a newspaper headline, something about the triumphant development of Hollywood and Technicolor, and immediately showing, at the bottom of the page, the almost imperceptible mention of the death of someone who had once been a star. That's how so many actors and actresses, once giants, are reduced to footnotes in the history of the all-consuming Hollywood machine.

1. See Frédéric Foubert, "Once Upon a Time in… Babylon. L'âge d'or selon Damien Chazelle," *Première*, January 2023.
2. With the exception of Gary Cooper, what most of these actors have in common is that they never successfully transitioned to talking films. John Gilbert (1897-1936), one of the great silent film actors, was an alcoholic and died of a heart attack at the age of 38. Douglas Fairbanks (1883-1939) quit acting in 1934 after making only four talking films and died five years later of a heart attack. Due to his strong accent, Danish-born actor Karl Dane (1886-1934) saw his career collapse with the advent of sound. He committed suicide at the age of 47. Max Linder (1883-1925), who suffered from depression, committed suicide after killing his wife.
3. Katherine Heslop and Paul F. Starrs, "The Gaming Zone: A One-Mile Limit at Stateline," *Yearbook of the Association of Pacific Coast Geographers*, vol. 74, 2012.
4. Gilles Deleuze, *Cinema 2: The Time-Image* (Minnesota, 1989), 192.
5. Arbuckle was suspected of sexually assaulting Virginia Rappe with a Coca-Cola or champagne bottle, or crushing her under his 265-pound weight, but the autopsy revealed that the victim had succumbed to a ruptured bladder followed by peritonitis, which occurred prior to the alleged assault. Despite his acquittal, the actor's reputation was permanently tarnished. Struggling with alcoholism, he died of a heart attack in 1933. See Greg Merritt, *Room 1219: The Life of Fatty Arbuckle, the Mysterious Death of Virginia Rappe, and the Scandal That Changed Hollywood* (Chicago Review Press, 2013).
6. See T.A. Frank, "The Alleged Trump-Putin 'Golden Shower' Fiasco, Explained," *Vanity Fair*, January 2017.
7. Simon Cherner, "Paul Verhoeven scandalisé de la pudibonderie de *Mourir peut attendre*," *Le Figaro*, 14 April 2022.

CODA

It's mid-January, almost a month since Babylon *was released in American cinemas, and the film is now beginning its European journey. You have just finished a series of premieres which took you to London, Paris and Rome. If you're willing, I would like to revisit the rather mixed critical reception the film received across the Atlantic. Were there any warning signs?*

There's always a risk – especially with a film like this – of drawing disapproval from the audience and facing criticism. I wasn't surprised, although I was, of course, hoping for the opposite.

Some reviews, like the one in The New York Times, *are harsh.[1] One recurring argument is about the "historical approximation."*

The moment you start digging into the unexpected or controversial aspects of something, which challenge the typical or accepted view, there are always people who consider themselves "experts" and get all bent out of shape.

What specific "historical approximations" are they referring to?

The extensive use of cocaine, which they say wasn't as prevalent in Hollywood in the 1920s and '30s as compared to opium, heroin and morphine.

I've read that in several articles, but it isn't true. Although *Babylon* isn't a documentary, it was important for me that everything depicted in the film – except for the intentional anachronisms in the dialogue or music – was based on reality.

What are your sources?

I had access to the photographic archives of the Getty and I read numerous books about the period, including the memoirs of Louise Brooks and biographies of Clara Bow, Anna May Wong and John Gilbert. Several books were particularly useful to me: the memoirs of playwright and screenwriter Frederica Sagor Maas[2]; *Hollywood Bohemians*, which deals with clubs and sexual deviations before World War II[3]; *Star-Dust in Hollywood*, an offbeat travelogue by a couple of British writers about a trip to California[4]; *Becoming Mexican American*, a study of the Hispanic community in Los Angeles[5]; *West of Eden*, an oral history of the pioneers of Los Angeles[6]; and *The Mirage Factory*, which focuses on three founding figures of the city – David W. Griffith, William Mulholland, the builder of the city's first aqueduct, and the evangelist Aimee Semple McPherson.[7] I also consulted Kevin Brownlow's books, especially *The Parade's Gone By*, and the *Hollywood* television series he made in 1980, which is full of interviews with actors and directors from the silent film era. Among the many books that deal with the transition from silent to sound film, perhaps the most useful was Scott Eyman's *The Speed of Sound*.[8] I also read historian Donald Bogle on blacks in Hollywood.[9] To be completely exhaustive, among my sources were novels of the time – by Raymond Chandler, John Fante and Nathanael West – and other books I found entertaining, if not absolutely rigorous in terms of historical accuracy, like *Hollywood Confidential*,[10] about connections between the film industry and the mafia, and books specifically about particular cases, like the murder of William Desmond Taylor[11] and the death of Virginia Rappe.[12] And it wasn't just written sources. On YouTube are a whole bunch of old promotional films about the studios, in which technicians can be seen working on sets built next to each other. I watched films made for the Los Angeles tourism office about restaurants and the city's architecture, and, of course, reports on movie premieres.

How did you go about making selections from that mass of material?

I wasn't interested in showcasing things we've all seen in films a thousand times already. I was interested in uncovering surprising anecdotes that challenged the typical view of Hollywood in the 1920s, which I highlight in *Babylon*. I wouldn't want to engage in cheap psychology, but maybe piling up these stories in one film is uncomfortable for people who have a fixed idea of the era. They don't want to entertain the possibility that it could all have been significantly different, because that would mean admitting they got it wrong, which is a tough pill to swallow.

That's the risk of a one-sided interpretation of history, even though we well know that historians tell stories "that they mark out at will through the very objective field of events," unable to capture the entirety of the events they describe, "for an itinerary cannot take every road." Paul Veyne – who I'm quoting here – concludes: "none of these itineraries is the true one, is History."[13]

As the son of a historian, I'm in a perfect position to know this.

I assume Babylon *also benefited from the expertise of historical consultants?*

It did. Our co-producer, Padraic Murphy, who heads a research company, also served as our assistant, and he connected us with specialists like Sherwin Dunner, a collector who was always sending us documents, and historian William F. Deverell,[14] who read various drafts of the script and gave feedback while we were editing. Each department, from costumes to cinematography, drew on its own specific research.

You mentioned the anachronisms. Even though the character of Nellie LaRoy is inspired by Clara Bow, I was struck by her modern appearance when she arrives at Don Wallach's party. It's as if she's from another era.

That's a good observation. Margot and I envisioned the character as if she came from the future or even from another planet. Nellie LaRoy is like an outsider crashing into a world she doesn't belong to, causing chaos wherever she goes. But we did try to strike a balance between taking creative liberties and staying true to the historical context. For instance, despite what some articles say, Nellie's costumes and hairstyles are based on real 1920s photographs, even though they might sometimes seem out of sync with that period. We opted for unconventional outfits and hairdos while aiming to keep the history intact. It's true that Nellie has a very anachronistic way of dancing, although some of her moves are inspired by some trends that were popular at the time. We also made sure she used some of the slang from that era, but her way of speaking sometimes has a modern twist. In the end, we were trying to figure out how to fit a character who doesn't naturally belong to that time into a period film. This challenge was particularly evident in the scene at William Randolph Hearst's party, where all the classic period film clichés come to life, but characters like Nellie and Sidney Palmer are like fish out of water. Through them, I wanted to show the process by which a society becomes its own cliché.

Aside from criticisms specifically about historical accuracy, Babylon was also attacked on artistic grounds. Some criticised its "ugliness," "unsexy" aesthetic, and "grotesque," "vulgar" or even "disgusting" aspects – descriptors that were used to ridicule Paul Verhoeven's Showgirls *upon its release, before the film was rehabilitated and became a "beloved political statement."*[15]

Perhaps, but the reception of *Showgirls* was in a league of its own compared to *Babylon*. Verhoeven's film was treated extremely harshly – totally unjustified in my opinion. There were no positive reviews, and it wasn't in the running for any awards, unlike mine. Due to its mixed reception, *Babylon* will likely need additional revenue sources to recoup its cost, but I hope it will gain value over time within Paramount's catalogue and eventually be profitable for the studio.

So it's not necessarily the commercial failure predicted by some observers?

The term "failure" gives me pause because it fuels this mistaken idea in film culture today that the value or success of a film should be measured only by its box-office take or the reviews it gets, rather than by the conversations it generates or the ripple effects it might produce on other filmmakers. Of course, I would have liked it if more people had gone to see *Babylon*. From a financial standpoint, it didn't do well in America.[16] At the same time, this underperformance is inexorably the fate of many year-end films, except for adaptations and franchises. The reality is clear: very few "adult" films succeeded commercially in the United States in 2022.

Do you attribute this to the proliferation of franchises?

It seems important to specify which franchises we're referring to. *Avatar*, for instance, is the work of a genuine *auteur*. The issue is undoubtedly more complex than it might initially seem. It's true that if you look at the state of criticism in the United States over the last twenty years, it tends to punish ambition, reject experimentation, and favour blockbusters. I hold it partly responsible for Marvel's dominance. It's the untold story: for each new film in the franchise, the critics – those same critics who reject half of the films in competition at every Cannes Film Festival – are unanimous, or nearly so. Existing as a filmmaker in a world where Marvel films, even though they don't need it, get better reviews than James Gray, Bruno Dumont or Gaspar Noé, is a real challenge. There are plenty of excellent critics who do their job very well. It's easy nowadays to be nostalgic about Pauline Kael and Andrew Sarris, but remember, they both hated Kubrick! [*laughs*] I don't want to generalise, but since maybe the late 2000s there's been a sort of resistance among critics whenever something deviates from the norm. As for *Babylon*, the reviews in England and France were good.

Overall, there are more positive reviews than negative in the French press,[17] although I sense a reluctance at major publications like Cahiers du cinéma *or* Positif[18] *to accept the complex and audacious approach to cinema that you champion.*

I've always tended to believe that French film criticism is on another level compared to American film criticism, but maybe I'm mistaken. What you're saying reminds me of an anecdote. Back when I was a student, Bruno Dumont came to Harvard to present *Twentynine Palms*. He gave a speech and spoke to students afterwards. Someone asked him, "What do you think about critics?" He said, "I'm always at war with criticism. It's a perpetual struggle." At first, I took this response as a provocation. Bruno Dumont, enfant terrible of French cinema, spurning institutionalised criticism! But later, when I read the reviews of *L'Humanité* and *Twentynine Palms*, which clearly seem to be extraordinary films, I understood what he meant. It's not so much that critics gave bad reviews to his films, which is part of the game. They *mocked* them, with an unbearable superiority. That's when I lost my illusions about criticism.

Nevertheless, I am indebted to critics as much as to filmmakers. Reading the work of Jonathan Rosenbaum, Pauline Kael, André Bazin and the writers from the old

Cahiers du cinéma has been as formative as watching Hitchcock, Truffaut and Eisenstein. Deep down, I know that good critics play a vital role in the development of art.

Can I go back to questions of economics? Besides the issue of franchises, in recent years we've seen strategies that have intensified with the Covid-19 pandemic, like releasing films simultaneously in cinemas and on streaming platforms, or producing movies exclusively for streaming services, which are attracting major filmmakers. Does that concern you?

Of course, yes. At the same time, I understand the allure that platforms hold for filmmakers. Releasing a film online means that the potential failure of a cinema release can be avoided. The economics are different, and platforms may be more open to experimentation. But for me, there's not much of a choice. Instead of making a film for a streaming platform, why not do something entirely different – like write a novel? Making a film is already so challenging. If we shoot a theatrical feature film to be seen anywhere other than a cinema, in other words anywhere other than under optimal conditions, what's the point? I would rather take the risk of a cinema release, even if it's just for three or four viewers who show up, than see my film exclusively streamed online. I might come across as a dinosaur, but from my perspective the initial experience of a film happens on the big screen. Home viewing, which I have nothing against – it's an integral part of cinephilia – comes later.

I sense that you're not buying into the doomsday talk of "cinema is dead," which certainly isn't a new idea,[19] but got a boost during the coronavirus pandemic and successive lockdowns. Is a film like Babylon *– also a story of death and rebirth – a way of reminding us of the vitality of cinema, its ability to reinvent itself and capacity to accommodate all kinds of different images and aesthetics,[20] as suggested by the epilogue?*

Definitely. Cinema's strength is in its messiness, as we've discussed, and perhaps with *Babylon* I tried to encompass *all* of cinema, like Godard did with his *Histoire(s) du cinéma*. But I don't want to reduce *Babylon*'s epilogue to just that. As with the end of all my previous films, there's a mix of fulfilment and tragedy. Being part of something greater. But at what cost? I appreciate the different reactions that *Babylon* elicits. Some will say the journey was worth it, others will remember the suffering that Hollywood wrought – the wasted lives, the sacrifices made by all these men and women who so desperately wanted to succeed. It's like cinema is a drug you can't quit. At the end, facing the screen, Manny weeps... but still craves more. This paradox is that of cinema itself, which, like any art, is the sum of creation and destruction.

---

1. Manohla Dargis, "Boozing. Snorting. That's Entertainment!?" *The New York Times*, 22 December 2022.
2. Frederica Sagor Maas, *The Shocking Miss Pilgrim: A Writer in Early Hollywood* (Kentucky, 1999).
3. Brett L. Abrams, *Hollywood Bohemians: Transgressive Sexuality and the Selling of the Modern Dream* (McFarland, 2008).
4. Jan Gordon and Cora Josephine Gordon, *Star-Dust in Hollywood* (G.G. Harrap, 1930).
5. George J. Sánchez, *Becoming Mexican American: Ethnicity, Culture, and Identity in Chicano Los Angeles, 1900-1945* (Oxford, 1995).
6. Jean Stein, *West of Eden: An American Place* (Random House, 2016).
7. Gary Krist, *The Mirage Factory: Illusion, Imagination, and the Invention of Los Angeles* (Broadway, 2019).
8. Scott Eyman, *The Speed of Sound: Hollywood and the Talkie Revolution, 1926-1930* (Simon & Schuster, 1997).
9. Donald Bogle, *Hollywood Black: the Stars, the Films, the Filmmakers* (Running Press Adult, 2019).
10. Ted Schwarz, *Hollywood Confidential: How the Studios Beat the Mob at Their Own Game* (Taylor Trade, 2007).
11. William J. Mann, *Tinseltown: Murder, Morphine and Madness at the Dawn of Hollywood* (HarperCollins, 2015).
12. Greg Merritt, *Room 1219: The Life of Fatty Arbuckle, the Mysterious Death of Virginia Rappe, and the Scandal that Changed Hollywood* (Chicago Review Press, 2013).
13. Paul Veyne, *Writing History* (Wesleyan, 1984), 36.
14. Among Deverall's notable works are *Whitewashed Adobe: The Rise of Los Angeles and the Remaking of Its Mexican Past* (California, 2004) and, with Tom Sitton, *Water and Los Angeles: A Tale of Three Rivers, 1900-1941* (California, 2017).
15. Jean-Marc Lalanne, "Réhabilitation: *Showgirls* de Paul Verhoeven n'est plus un navet!" *Les Inrocks*, 14 September 2016.

16. During its opening weekend in December 2022, *Babylon* was screened at more than 3,300 cinemas across the United States and grossed only about $3.5 million dollars. Besides a lukewarm critical reception, two other factors might explain this number: the dominance of James Cameron's *Avatar: The Way of Water* at the box office, and a winter storm that paralysed parts of the country.
17. As examples, and without aiming for completeness: *Babylon* was featured on the cover of *Première* (January 2023); Emmanuel Tellier raved ("*Babylon*, un miracle à Hollywood?" *Marianne*, 12-18 January 2023); Philippe Guedj gave it four out of five stars in *Le Point* (12 January 2023); *Cinémateaser* published an insightful interview with Damien Chazelle (Renan Cros, "*Babylon*, de bruit et de fureur," December 2022/January 2023); Frédéric Strauss praised Margot Robbie's performance, stating that she "shines as a silent film star" (*Télérama*, 17 January 2023). Note also Dork Zabunyan, "Reconstituer ou reconstruire Hollywood? Notes aqueuses sur *Babylon* de Damien Chazelle," *Palm*, April-December 2023.
18. See Charlotte Garson, "Hollywood cannibal," *Cahiers du cinéma*, January 2023, and Emmanuel Raspiengeas, "Once Upon a Time in Hollywoodland," *Positif*, January 2023. There are other critical reviews on the website of *Le Masque et la Plume*.
19. See Antoine de Baecque, *Le cinéma est mort, vive le cinéma! L'histoire-caméra II* (Gallimard, 2021).
20. Jacques Rancière, *La Méthode de l'égalité* (Bayard, 2012), 247.

LYRICS

Guy and Madeline on a Park Bench
Music by Justin Hurwitz, lyrics by Damien Chazelle

Cincinnati

I left my heart in Cincinnati
Queen Anne Avenue, two blocks away
In the dark, where we used to hold hands
And the picture show used to play
I left my heart in Cincinnati
When the lights come on, the show did end
And there we were, my lovelorn baby
Maybe one day we'll meet again

Love in the Fall

Love in the fall
There ain't no lovin' at all
June's curtain drops, the romance stops

And so, I bright and spry
My lonely lover's eye
Will search under the leaves
For a love that blinks and breathes

Here I am, in the fall
There ain't no lovin' at all
Red branches hang over the mass

And below, they come and go
In their mood indigo
Seek and you shall find
Unless you're of the romantic kind

Oh love in the fall

Love in the fall
There ain't no lovin' at all
Cupid's as harmless as a dove

And below them come and go
In their mood indigo
Hello fall, thanks for the call
And bye, bye love

It Happened at Dawn

It happened at dawn
Happened in this park
A guy and girl had dallied 'till the moon was gone

Then it sprang
And up the moment came
The sun's to blame
Their love happened at dawn

They'd met the night before
The water's shore
He played his horn across the park

And so they strolled
And spoke of years of old
Back when the folks would dance in the dark

They found a place to sit where all the lamps were lit
Their fingers grazed
Hands almost touched so long

Then the sun arose and split the mist
The guy and girl, they stole a kiss
It happened at the break of dawn
Right at dawn

She slipped through his hands
She felt like sand
She wondered if her face was sweet enough

He dove in
He kissed her with a grin

But wondered if his lips felt too rough

Then the sun began its morning run
The fountain won
They thought it might be time to take a chance

Start a new life
With a new romance

"Yes all love fades away"
That's what folks like to say
But these two kids, they knew that line was wrong

When they said fair love would stay alive
It'd grow until the day they died
It happened at the break of dawn

Je savais pas

Je savais pas qu'un jour
Il m'arriverait de trouver
Une fille aussi belle que toi,
Que toi

Pas n'importe-quoi n'importe-qui
Ne m'aurait dit
Que tu viendrais sous mon toit,
Mon toit

Mon cœur éclate à bout de souffle
Je cours afin de te rejoindre
Ah oui je cours
Mon amour

Pourrais-je oublier le moment
Où l'on s'est rencontrés,
Toi et moi,
Il y a un jour

Là j'ai vu une fille de poésie
Des bijoux dans ses yeux
C'est la plus belle chanson d'amour,
D'amour

Ma destinée est décidée
Cette fille qui s'appelle Madeleine
A rendu un pauv' malheureux,
Heureux

Une vendeuse de fleurs
Qui ne voit pas
M'a laissé sans un choix
Oui c'est toi

Maintenant cette Madeleine
Conjure des souvenirs,
Des souvenirs

Souvenirs d'une autre fille,
D'une fille qui s'appelait Sophie,
Sophie

The Boy in the Park

Dancing
Yes I was dancin'
With angels who'd come down on a lark
And what's funny, I think I found a spark
When I kissed the boy in the park

Dancin'
Just romancin'
And prancin' to cherries on the trees
And what's funny, it was just a little breeze
If I'd been standin' it'd have knocked me on my knees

Oh I like New York in the fall
When Esther sings, and dogs in love bark
But it just can't compare to that waltz in the air
When I kissed the boy in the park

Dancin'
Oh yes, I was dancin'

Dancin'
Yes you were dancin'
And prancin' to cherries on the trees
And what's funny, it was just a little breeze
If I'd been standin' it'd have knocked me on my knees

Oh, I like New York in the fall
When Esther sings, and dogs in love bark
But it just can't compare to that waltz in the air
When I kissed the boy in the park

Oh how I like a foggy winter's day
And city lights writing in the dark
But neither can compete, 'cause my heart skipped a beat
When I kissed the boy in the park

The boy in the park!

Babylon
Music by Justin Hurwitz, lyrics by Damien Chazelle

I want a man, I want a man, I do
I want a man, I want a man
I want a hunky-dunky, chunky man
I want a man, I want a man

I want a man who'll rub my back at night
With his big and hairy hands
I want a strong man, caveman, one-man band
They will say, "Oh, what a man"

I want a man who wants me in the kitchen
Cooking him his sausage in a pan
I want a man who wants me in the bedroom
Shaking my sweet titties like a flan

I want a man who wants me in the kitchen
Cooking him his sausage in a pan
I want a man who wants me in the bedroom
Shaking my sweet titties like a flan

I want a man, I want a man, I do
I want a man, I want a man
I want a purty, flirty, dirty man
Please hear me, God, I want a man

ACKNOWLEDGEMENTS

This book would not have been possible without the generosity, availability and trust of Damien Chazelle. I would like to express my deep gratitude to him.

My warmest thanks go to Celia and Bernard Chazelle, who enthusiastically welcomed this project, and to my colleague and friend Éric Palazzo, who initiated this wonderful adventure. I'm grateful to all three of them for their passionate, attentive and rigorous scrutiny of the first draft of my manuscript, and in particular to Celia for her pertinent comments on the English translation.

Many thanks to Daniel McFadden for use of the cover photograph.

This publishing adventure would not have been possible without the commitment of Guy Astic, director of Éditions Rouge Profond, and Paul Cronin, director of Sticking Place Books, to whom I express my sincere gratitude for his fine translation of the original manuscript, and for giving it new visibility across the Atlantic.

Thanks to my dear wife and to my closest friends for their unconditional support.

Paul Cronin would like to extend thanks to Stacey Knecht for assistance with the translation and production of this book.

INDEX

8 femmes (Ozon), 22
8½ (Fellini), 139
10 Cloverfield Lane (Trachtenberg) 37-38, 42n
400 Blows, The (Truffaut), 44
2001: A Space Odyssey (Kubrick), 101, 147

Abbott, Christopher, 113n
Abiteboul, Olivier, 7
Abrams, J.J., 38
A Christmas Carol (Marin), 31
A Day in the Country (Renoir)
Adorno, Theodor W., 53-54, 57
Adventures of Robin Hood, The, (Curtiz/Keighley), 83
Affleck, Casey, 105
Akerman, Chantal, 23, 32n
Aldrin, Buzz, 98, 103, 109
Alighieri, Dante, 135
All My Life (Baillie), 33
Almendros, Néstor, 59
Amants du Pont-Neuf, Les (Carax), 34
American Hustle (Russell), 74
An American in Paris (Minnelli), 24

Anderson, Paul Thomas, 139
Anderson, Perry, 86, 89n
Anger, Kenneth, 137
À nos amours (Pialat), 32n
Apocalypse Now (Coppola), 130
Apollo 11 (Miller), 99
Apollo 13 (Howard), 93, 113n
A Prophet (Audiard), 120
Arbuckle, Roscoe C. "Fatty", 139-40, 149n
Armstrong, Neil, 4-5, 62, 93-94, 96, 98, 100-102, 104-108, 122
Arrival (Villeneuve), 88, 107-8
Arzner, Dorothy, 136
Astaire, Fred, 72, 74, 79
Astic, Guy, 1
A Streetcar Named Desire (Kazan), 16
A Trip to the Moon (Méliès), 147
Audiard, Jacques, 120
Avatar (Cameron), 147, 155
Avatar: The Way of Water (Cameron), 159n
A Woman is a Woman (Godard), 23

Bacall, Lauren, 72

172 Playing Among the Stars

Bach, Johann Sebastian, 29, 99
Baillie, Bruce, 33
Ballard, Glen, 116, 119
Ballard, Jeff, 31n
Ballet Mécanique
   (Léger/Murphy), 28
Balzac, Honoré de, 81
Band Wagon, The (Minnelli), 24, 86
Barry Lyndon (Kubrick), 33, 144
Barton Fink (Coen Brothers), 146
Bassett, Charles, 94
Battleship Potemkin (Eisenstein), 48
Baudelaire, Charles, 65n, 141
Bazin, André, 48, 60, 61, 65n, 156
Beat That My Heart Skipped, The
   (Audiard), 49-50
Beatty, Warren, 88
Beau travail (Denis), 34
Bechet, Sidney, 125n, 136
Becker, Jacques, 35
Becoming Mexican American
   (Sánchez), 152
Beeswax (Bujalski), 30
Beethoven, Ludwig van, 141
Before Sunset (Linklater), 23
Beiderbecke, Bix, 54
Bekhti, Leïla, 120
Benjamin, Arthur, 40
Benyamina, Houda, 117-18, 123
Bergman, Ingmar, 36
Best Years of Our Lives, The
   (Wyler) 89n
Biancosino, Anthony J., 17-18, 45, 55-57
Bird (Eastwood), 58
Black and Tan Fantasy (Murphy), 28
Black Narcissus (Powell/
   Pressburger), 83
Blakey, Art, 17, 125n
Blanchett, Cate, 65n
Blood of the Beasts (Franju), 20, 33
Blue is the Warmest Colour
   (Kechiche), 34
Bogart, Humphrey, 72
Bogle, Donald, 152
Bolden, Buddy, 54
Bonnie and Clyde (Penn), 16
Bow, Clara, 136, 146, 152, 154
Brakhage, Stan, 20, 159, 147

Brahms, Johannes, 29
Bridesmaids (Feig), 143
Brody, Richard, 56-57
Brooks, Louise, 138, 141, 152
Brownlow, Kevin, 152
Brueghel, Pieter, 141
Bujalski, Andrew, 30, 32n
Buñuel, Luis, 127, 147
Burger, Fred, 36
Burn After Reading (Coen
   Brothers), 131

Cabin in the Sky (Minnelli), 24
Calva, Diego, 5, 133,
Cameron, James, 147, 159n
Campbell, Josh, 38
Cantet, Laurent, 34
Carax, Leos, 34
Cardiff, Jack, 83
Cardona, René, 136
Carmichael, Hoagy, 68, 89n
Carné, Marcel, 125n
Cartland, Barbara, 86
Casablanca (Curtiz), 87, 89n
Cassavetes, John, 2, 21, 23, 25-27, 32n, 123, 139
Castelnuovo, Nino, 82
Casualites of War (De Palma), 51, 52, 65n
Catlett, Sidney, 17, 54
Chaffee, Roger, 94
Chagall, Marc, 82
Chandler, Raymond, 152
Chansons d'amour, Les (Honoré), 22
Chaplin, Charles, 23, 27-28, 32n, 61, 135, 141
Charles, Ray, 89n
Chastain, Jessica, 70
Chaucer, Geoffrey, 141
Chester French (band), 19, 73
Chevalier, Maurice, 23
Chronicle of a Summer (Rouch/
   Morin), 20, 33
Cinderella (Disney), 13
Citizen Kane (Welles), 33
City Lights (Chaplin), 27, 33
Clarke, Arthur C., 112
Clarke, Jason, 103
Clarke, Kenny, 54
Clarke, Shirley, 26
Clay, Sonny, 136

Cléo de 5 à 7 (Varda), 23
Close-Up (Kiarostami), 34
Cloverfield (Reeves), 37-38, 42n
Cloverfield Paradox, The (Onah), 42n
Clowns, The (Fellini), 139
Coen Brothers, 131, 134
Cold War (Pawlikowski), 120
Coleman, Bill, 125n
College (Horne/Keaton), 27
Collins, Michael, 103
Containment (Moss/Galison), 32n
Coltrane, John, 54, 68
Comencini, Luigi, 78
Computer Chess (Bujalski), 32n
Constantin, Jean, 44
Cooper, Gary, 131, 149n
Coppola, Francis Ford, 8, 92, 128, 134
Cornell, Joseph, 20
Cosmopolis (Cronenberg), 78
Couperin, François, 70
Cousteau, Jacques-Yves, 101
Crash (Cronenberg), 78
Crazy, Stupid, Love (Ficarra/Requa), 72
Crewdson, Gregory, 82
Crisis (Drew), 116
Cronenberg, David, 78
Cross, Tom, 35, 62-63, 107
Crowe, Cameron, 68
Crowley, Nathan, 97
Crown, The (TV), 102
Cukor, George, 31n

Dancer in the Dark (von Trier), 76
Dane, Karl, 131, 149n
Daney, Serge, 60
David Copperfield (Cukor), 31n
Davis, Miles, 26, 68
De Palma, Brian, 8, 39, 51, 60-61, 65n, 113n
Dead Man's Bones (band), 89n
Dekalogue, The (Kieslowski), 34
Delerue, Georges, 44
Deleuze, Gilles, 27, 32n, 149n
Demy, Jacques, 2, 21-22, 27, 32n, 44, 76, 80, 83
Deneuve, Catherine, 82
Denis, Claire, 34
Deverell, William F., 154
Disney, Walt, 13, 59

Dodds, Baby, 54
Donen, Stanley, 79
Double Life of Veronique, The (Kieslowski), 34
Douchet, Jean, 9n
Drew, Robert, 116
Dreyer, Carl Theodor, 33
Drummey, Maxwell, 19
Ducastel, Olivier, 22
Duhamel, Antoine, 44
Duke, Charles, 106
Dumont, Bruno, 156
Dunaway, Faye, 88
Dunkirk (Nolan), 97
Dunner, Sherwin, 154
Duris, Romain, 50

East of Borneo (Melford), 20
Eastwood, Clint, 58, 93
Eco, Umberto, 86-87, 139
Edwards, Blake, 8
Eggleston, William, 82
Eisenstein, Sergei, 48, 157
Ellington, Duke, 29, 44, 55
Emperor Jones, The (Murphy), 28
Eyes Wide Shut (Kubrick), 8, 85-86, 139
Eyman, Scott, 152

Fairbanks, Douglas, 131, 149n
Falconetti, Renée, 141
Fantasia (Disney), 59
Fante, John, 152
Fargo (Coen Brothers), 34
Feig, Eric, 37
Fellini, Federico, 8, 44, 139
Ferré, Léo, 125n
Field, Todd, 65n
Fingers (Toback), 49
Flaubert, Gustave, 8
For All Mankind (Reinert), 93
Ford, John, 32n
Fox, Michael J., 52
Foy, Claire, 102
Franju, Georges, 33
French Connection, The (Friedkin), 64
Friedkin, William, 64
Fuller, Samuel, 32n, 58
Full Metal Jacket (Kubrick), 51

Galison, Peter, 32n

Gangster Squad (Fleischer), 72
Garbo, Greta, 61, 138
Garcia, Desiree, 20, 29
Garland, Judy, 72
Gass-Donnelly, Ed, 37
Gautier, Éric, 123
Gazzara, Ben, 123
Gervais, Ricky, 115
Gilbert, John, 131, 146, 149n, 152
Gillespie, Dizzy, 54
Gimme Shelter (Maysles), 21, 116
Gish, Lillian, 138
Godard, Jean-Luc, 20, 23, 27-29, 33, 44, 59-60, 78, 158
Godfather, The (Coppola), 8, 128
Godfather, The, Part III (Coppola), 92
Godfrey, Wyck, 93
Gone With the Wind (Fleming), 83
Goodman, Benny, 54-55
Goodman, John, 38
Gordon, Dexter, 26
Gosling, Ryan, 4, 69, 71-74, 76, 89, 101-102, 104
Grand Piano (Mira), 37, 39-42
Grant, Cary, 61
Gray, James, 9n, 34, 63, 156
Greed (von Stroheim), 92
Griffith, D.W., 6, 8, 138, 147, 152
Grissom, Virgil "Gus", 94
Guattari, Félix, 27

Haas, Lukas, 103
Hackman, Gene, 64
Hallelujah, I'm a Bum (Milestone), 23
Hamilton, Olivia, 35, 103, 129
Hampton, Lionel, 125n
Hancock, Herbie, 31n
Hangover, The (Phillips), 141
Hansen, James R., 93, 104, 106
Harold & Kumar (Leiner), 141
Haut bas fragile (Rivette), 23
Hawks, Howard, 89n
Hearst, William Randolph, 136, 154
Henderson, Fletcher, 55
Herrmann, Bernard, 40
High Flying Bird (Soderbergh), 124
High School (Wiseman), 20
Histoire(s) du cinéma (Godard), 158

Hitchcock, Alfred, 15, 19, 26, 33, 39-40, 61, 84, 147, 157
Hockney, David, 82, 89n
Hoffman, Samuel J., 96
Holland, André, 115, 120, 123, 131
Holliday, Billie, 116
Hollywood (documentary, 1980), 152
Hollywood (mini-series, 2020), 137
Hollywood Bohemians (Abrams), 152
Hollywood Confidential (Schwartz), 152
Homer, 102
Honoré, Christophe, 22
Hopper, Edward, 82
Horowitz, Jordan, 36
Hospital (Wiseman), 20
Hour of the Furnaces, The (Getino/Solanas), 20
Howard, Ron, 93, 113n
Humanité, L (Dumont), 156
Hurwitz, Justin, 2, 4, 19, 29-30, 35, 43-44, 65n, 73, 79, 96, 104, 161, 167
Hutton, Peter, 20

Inglourious Basterds (Tarantino), 131
Inside Llewyn Davis (Coen Brothers), 34
Interstellar (Nolan), 97
Intolerance (Griffith), 8, 147
It's Always Fair Weather (Kelly/Donen), 24
I Vitelloni (Fellini), 139

James, Harry, 55
Jazz Dance (Tilton/Leacock), 21
Jazz on a Summer's Day (Stern/Avakian), 116
Jeanne et le garçon formidable (Ducastel/Martineau), 22
Jenkins, Barry, 87
Jerry Maguire (Crowe), 68
Jolson, Al, 23
Jones, Elvin, 17
Jones, Jo, 17, 56-58
Jonze, Spike, 63
Joy (Russell), 74
Juno (Reitman), 51

Kael, Pauline, 156
Kaleta, Kelly, 29
Kalmus, Natalie, 83
Kaufman, Philip, 93
Kazan, Elia, 20
Keaton, Buster, 27-28
Kelly, Gene, 8, 21-22, 24, 76,
Kerber, Randy
Khin, Sandha, 24
Kiarostami, Abbas, 25, 34
Kid, The (Chaplin), 142
Kierkegaard, Søren, 7
Kieslowski, Krzysztof, 34
Killing of a Chinese Bookie, The
 (Cassavetes), 123
Klausner, Isaac, 93
Knight of Cups (Malick), 71
Konitz, Lee, 31n
Krupa, Gene, 17
Kubrick, Stanley, 8, 19, 33, 51, 85,
 101, 112, 143-44, 156
Kulig, Joanna, 120

La dolce vita (Fellini), 139
L'Âge d'or (Buñuel), 127
Lambert, Paul, 97
Lancaster, Burt, 131
Lang, Nate, 46
Last Exorcism, The (Stamm), 37
Last Exorcism: Part II, The
 (Gass-Donnelly), 37
Lawrence of Arabia (Lean), 130
Leacock, Richard, 21
Lean, David, 141
Led Zeppelin, 55
Lee, Spike, 24
Legend, John, 73
Léger, Fernand, 28
Legrand, Michel, 2, 29, 44, 80, 88
Leguizamo, John, 51-52
Leone, Sergio, 6, 44, 97, 128
Léonnet, Natasha, 84
Leopard, The (Visconti), 131
Levy, Hank, 44
Linder, Max, 131, 149n
Linklater, Richard, 23
Lonergan, Kenneth, 105
Louis, Ludovic, 119-20
Love Me Tonight (Mamoulian),
 23, 75
Loy, Myrna, 72
Luciano, Charles "Lucky," 136

Magnificent Ambersons, The
 (Welles), 92
Maguire, Tobey, 135
Maisler, Francine, 102
Malick, Terrence, 34, 69-71
Mamoulian, Rouben, 23, 142
Manchester By the Sea (Lonergan),
 105
Man Who Knew Too Much, The
 (Hitchcock), 39-40
Marin, Edwin L., 31n
Marker, Chris, 20
Marrakchi, Laïla, 117-18
Marsalis, Wynton, 31n
Martin, John, 14, 31n
Martineau, Jacques, 22
Marx Brothers, 127, 145
Mastroianni, Marcello, 131
Maupassant, Guy de, 77
Maysles, Albert, 20
Maysles, David, 20
McGlade, Jasmin, 30, 32n
McPherson, Aimee Semple, 152
Meet Me in St. Louis (Minnelli),
 79, 83
Melford, George, 20
Méliès, Georges, 147
Melville, Jean-Pierre, 35
Merchant, Stephen, 115
Méril, Macha, 88
Metropolis (Lang), 16
Milestone, Lewis, 23, 142
Miller, Todd Douglas, 99
Minnelli, Vincente, 24, 28, 61, 86
Mira, Eugenio, 39, 41-42
Mirage Factory, The (Krist), 152
Mission to Mars (De Palma), 113
Mitchell, John Cameron, 45
Monk, Thelonious, 56, 68
Monroe, Marilyn, 61
Monty Python, 146
Monty Python: The Meaning of
 Life (Jones/Gilliam), 143
Moonlight (Jenkins), 87
Moore, Mandy, 74, 76, 144
Morricone, Ennio, 44, 97
Mosby, Curtis, 136
Moss, Robb, 30, 32n
Mouëllic, Gilles, 3
Moullet, Luc, 58
Moussorgsky, Modeste

Mozart, Wolfgang Amadeus, 29, 59
Mud (Nichols), 70
Mulholland Drive (Lynch), 146
Mulholland, William, 152
Murphy, Dudley, 28, 34, 142
Murphy, Padraic, 154
Murphy, Ryan, 137
My Night at Maud's (Rohmer), 77

Nanook of the North (Flaherty), 20
National Lampoon's Animal House (Landis), 141
Newman, Eric, 37
New World, The (Malick), 34
Nichols, Jeff, 70
Nicholson, Jack, 131
Nietzsche, Friedrich, 5
Night Nurse (Wellman), 142
Noé, Gaspard, 156
Nolan, Christopher, 97-98, 130
Nueva, Damián, 119

O'Connor, Donald, 143
Obradovic, Lada, 119
Office, The (TV), 115
Old School (Phillips), 141
Omicil, Jowee, 119
Onah, Julius, 42n
Once Upon a Time... in Hollywood (Tarantino), 131-32
Once Upon a Time in the West (Leone), 97
Once Upon a Time in America (Leone), 128
On connaît la chanson (Resnais), 22
On the Town (Kelly/Donen), 24, 76, 79
On the Waterfront (Kazan), 20
Oppenheimer (Nolan), 130
Oz (TV), 51
Ozon, François, 22
Ozu, Yasujirô, 22

Pacino, Al, 134
Palmer, Jason, 20-21, 25-26, 31n, 136
Pandora's Box (Pabst), 141
Parker, Adam, 30
Parker, Charlie, 29, 54, 58

Party, The (Edwards), 8
Pasek, Benj, 80-81
Pasolini, Pier Paolo, 12, 146
Passion of Joan of Arc, The (Dreyer), 33, 141
Paul, Justin, 80-81
Pawlikowski, Pawel, 120
Peary, Gerald, 30, 32n
Penn, Sean, 51-52, 70
Pennies from Heaven (Ross), 76
Peter Pan (Disney), 13
Peterson, Oscar, 56
Petit soldat, Le (Godard), 60
Phantom Thread (Anderson), 139
Pialat, Maurice, 3, 25, 32n, 34
Pickford, Mary, 61
Pitt, Brad, 70, 81, 129, 131, 140
Platt, Marc, 129
Plouffe, Matthew, 35-36, 129
Post, The (Spielberg), 95
Poul, Alan, 116-17
Poupard, Julien, 118
Powell, Michael, 28, 83
Powell, William, 72
Pressburger, Emeric, 28, 83
Primary (Drew), 116
Psycho (Hitchcock), 147
Public Enemy, The (Wellman), 142
Pulp Fiction (Tarantino), 83
Puzo, Mario, 92

Rabbit Hole (Mitchell), 45-46
Rabelais, François, 141
Rashomon (Kurosawa), 16
Raging Bull (Scorsese), 57
Rahim, Tahar, 120
Rappe, Virginia, 139, 149n, 153
Ravel, Maurice, 144
Red Shoes, The (Powell/Pressburger), 83
Reeves, Matt, 37
Région Centrale, La (Snow), 20
Reinert, Al, 93
Reitman, Jason, 46, 51, 63
Renoir, Jean, 33, 77
Resnais, Alain, 22-23
Revel, Harry, 96
Reyes, Victor, 40
Rich, Buddy, 2, 17, 53, 56-57
Right Stuff, The (Kaufman), 93
Riverdogs (Moss), 32n
Rivette, Jacques, 23

Roach, Max, 17
Robbie, Margot, 5, 127, 129, 131-34, 159n
Robeson, Paul, 28
Rogers, Ginger, 72, 74-75, 79
Rohmer, Éric, 59, 77
Romanek, Mark, 63
Rooney, Mickey, 72
Rosenbaum, Jonathan, 156
Rose Hobart (Cornell), 20
Rota, Nino, 44
Roth, Eli, 37
Rouch, Jean, 26-27, 116
'Round Midnight (Tavernier), 26
Ruscha, Ed, 82, 89n
Russell, David O., 63, 74

Salesman (Maysles), 20
Salò, or the 120 Days of Sodom (Pasolini), 147
Same River Twice, The (Moss), 32
Sandgren, Linus, 35, 83-83, 97, 117
Sans soleil (Marker), 20
Sagor Maas, Frederica, 152
Sarris, Andrew, 156
Scarface (De Palma), 8
Scenes from a Marriage (Bergman), 36
Schamus, James, 35
Schubert, Franz, 144
Scorsese, Martin, 57
Scott, Dave, 98, 113n
Scott-Heron, Gil, 112, 114n
See, Elliot, 94
Sellers, Peter, 132, 145
Seven Brides for Seven Brothers (Donen), 24
Shadows (Cassavetes), 2, 21, 23, 31n
Shakespeare, William, 14, 68
Shaw, Artie, 55
Sherlock, Jr. (Keaton), 27
Sheridan, Tye, 70
She's Gotta Have It (Lee), 24
Showgirls (Verhoeven), 139-140, 155
Simmons, J. K., 46, 49, 51-52, 64, 81-82
Simmons, Johnny, 45
Simonec, Tim, 44, 65n
Singer, Josh, 95, 100, 195

Singin' in the Rain (Kelly/Donen), 8, 22, 34, 79, 138, 143, 146-57
Sirk, Douglas, 61
Skippy (Taurog), 9n
Snow, Michael, 20
Social Network, The (Fincher), 34
Soderbergh, Steven, 124
Solal, Martial, 44
Solanas, Fernando, 20
Solaris (Tarkovsky), 107
Some Like It Hot (Wilder), 16
Song to Song (Malick), 69, 71
Spears, Britney, 55
Speed of Sound, The (Eyman), 152
Spencer, Marie, 118
Spider-Man (Raimi), 51
Spielberg, Steven, 44, 63, 95-96
Stamm, Daniel, 37
Star-Dust in Hollywood (Gordon), 152
Stenberg, Amandla, 124
Stevenson, Robert, 31n
St. Louis Blues (Léger), 28
Stoll, Corey, 103
Stone, Emma, 4, 69, 72-76, 80-81, 87, 129, 132-33
Subor, Michel, 60
Suecken, Matt, 38
Summer Stock (Walter), 76
Sunset Boulevard (Wilder), 146

Tár (Field), 65n
Tarantino, Quentin, 32n, 83-83, 131
Tarkovsky, Andrei, 107
Tati, Jacques, 78
Tatum, Art, 41, 42n
Taubin, Amy, 30
Taurog, Norman, 9n
Tavernier, Bertrand, 26
Taylor, William Desmond, 153
Teller, Miles, 45-47, 49, 69, 89n
Thalberg, Irving, 136
Thelonious Monk: Straight, No Chaser (Zwerin), 21
There Will Be Blood (Anderson), 34
There's Something About Mary (Farrelly Brothers), 141
Thin Red Line, The (Malick), 34, 71
Thorne, Jack, 116, 121

Titanic (Cameron), 34
Tilton, Roger, 21
Time Out (Cantet), 34
Tizol, Juan, 44
Toback, James, 49
Todd, Thelma, 136
To Have and Have Not (Hawks), 89n
Tom Brown's School Days (Stevenson), 31n
Top Hat (Sandrich), 79
Tourist, The (Moss), 32n
To the Wonder (Malick), 71
Trachtenberg, Dan, 38
Trafic (Tati), 78
Traffic Jam (Comencini), 78
Tree of Life, The (Malick), 34, 70-71
Tricheurs, Les (Carné), 125n
Truffaut, François, 19, 44, 157
Trump, Donald, 109-110, 140
Tsai Ming-liang, 34
Twentynine Palms (Dumont), 156
Twilight Saga, The, 93
Two Lovers (Gray), 34

Umbrellas of Cherbourg, The (Demy), 22-23, 29, 33, 77, 82
Un Chien Andalou (Buñuel/Dali), 147
Ungar, Gary, 35
Unsane (Soderbergh), 124

Valentino, Rudolph, 61, 146
Vallejo, Enrique, 136
Varda, Agnès, 28, 88
Verhoeven, Paul, 139-41, 155
Verne, Jules, 101
Vertigo (Hitchcock), 33, 84-85
Veyne, Paul, 153
Vian, Boris, 125
Villeneuve, Denis, 88, 107
Visconti, Luchino, 134, 141
Vivre sa vie (Godard), 23, 33
Von Braun, Wernher, 110
Von Stroheim, Erich, 92, 136
Vonnegut, Kurt, 112
Voyage of Time (Malick), 71

Wachsberger, Patrick, 37
Wagner, Bob, 129
Wallach, D.A, 19, 73

Walters, Charles, 76
Ward Kelly, Patricia, 76
Wasco, David, 82-83
Wasco, Sandy, 82-83
Watson, Emma, 69-72
Webb, Chick, 17, 54
Weekend (Godard), 78
Welles, Orson, 26, 33, 92
Wellman, William, 142
West, Nathanael, 152
West of Eden (Stein), 152
White, Ed, 94, 103
White, Pat, 103
Wilder, Billy, 19
Williams, John, 44
Williams, Pharrell, 31n
Willis, Bruce, 83
Wings (Wellman), 142
Wiseman, Frederick, 2, 20, 24, 26
Wizard of Oz, The (Fleming), 98
Wong, Anna May, 136, 152
Wong Kar-wai, 34
Wyler, William, 89n

Yards, The (Gray), 34
Yeager, Chuck, 93
Young, Lester, 54, 116
Young and Innocent (Hitchcock), 40
Young Girls of Rochefort, The (Demy), 29, 36

Zabriskie Point (Antonioni), 148
Zophres, Mary, 83, 85
Zwerin, Charlotte, 21

www.ingramcontent.com/pod-product-compliance
Lightning Source LLC
Chambersburg PA
CBHW070141080526
44586CB00015B/1782